D0206662

TEACHINGS OF RUMI

Teachings of
RUMI

Re-created and edited by
ANDREW HARVEY

SHAMBHALA
Boston & London
1999

For

Gloria Vanderbilt Cooper

"Real lovers serve ardently, hopefully,

in an ecstasy of awe."

—Rumi

Shambhala Publications, Inc.
Horticultural Hall
300 Massachusetts Avenue
Boston, Massachusetts 02115
http://www.shambhala.com

9   8   7   6   5   4   3   2   1

FIRST EDITION
Printed in the United States of America

⊗ This edition is printed on acid-free paper that meets the
American National Standards Institute z39.48 Standard.
Distributed in the United States by Random House, Inc.,
and in Canada by Random House of Canada Ltd.

Library of Congress Cataloging-in-Publication Data
The Teaching of Rumi/edited by Andrew Harvey.—1st ed.
         p.   cm.
    ISBN 1-57062-346-5
    1. Jalāl al-Dīn Rūmī, Maulana, 1207–1273.   2. Mevleviyeh.
I. Harvey, Andrew, 1952–
BP189.7.M42T43   1999   98-54866
297.4'092—dc21   CIP

CONTENTS

PART II

Be a Lover

PART III

Ordeal

PART IV

Union

ACKNOWLEDGMENTS

To my Mother, for the inspiration of her love of truth.

To Eryk, my husband, bringer of fire and tender heart-companion.

To Leila and Henry Luce, for their constantly encouraging kindness.

To Mara and Joey Singer, for the truth of their friendship.

To Tracy Cochran, for her kind and generous help and witness.

To Tami Simon, for her clarity and integrity.

To Eva de Vitray Meyerovitch, for her pioneering work and for many hours of communion in the presence of Our Beloved.

To my editor, Dave O'Neal, for his support and vision.

To the blessed memory of Bella von Heinz, who first awoke me to the wonder of Islam.

INTRODUCTION

JALAL-UD-DIN RUMI, the greatest mystic of Islam, and, many people believe, of the world, was born in Balkh, Afghanistan on September 30, 1207, and died in Konya, Southern Turkey, on December 17, 1273. He left behind as the record of his extraordinarily intense life, lived on the wildest and grandest heights of the spirit, the *Mathnawi*, a mystical epic; 3,500 odes; 2,000 quatrains; a book of table talk; and a large volume of letters. The Mevlevi order that he founded and that was continued by his son, Sultan Valad, spread his vision all over Asia and Africa and now has centers all over the world.

In the last twenty years, through the pioneering translations of Coleman Barks, Robert Bly, Kabir Helminski, and Jonathan Star, among others, Rumi has become, as Bill Moyers pointed out in his recent television special on him, "the most popular poet in America," read and loved by seekers of all persuasions and creeds. For hundreds of thousands of people, Rumi's work in its passion, honesty, and gorgeous imagery has become a way of connecting directly with the Divine beyond the constrictions of religion or dogma. Rumi now commands in the West what he has long commanded in the East—an unassailable position as the most poignant and vibrant of all celebrators of the Path of Love and as a supreme witness, in a way that transcends all national, cultural, and religious boundaries, to the mysteries of Divine Identity and Presence.

Rumi combined the intellect of a Plato, the vision and enlightened soul-force of a Buddha or a Christ, and the extravagant literary gifts of a Shakespeare. This unique fusion of the highest philosophical lucidity with the greatest possible spiritual awareness and the most complete artistic gifts give Rumi unique power as what might be called a Sacred Initiator or Initiator into the Sacred. Born out of the fire of a vast Awakening, Rumi's work has an uncanny direct force of illumination; anyone approaching it with an open heart and mind, at whatever stage of his or her evolution, will derive from it inspiration, excitement, and help of the highest kind. Everything Rumi wrote or transmitted has the unmistakable authority of total inner experience, the authority of a human being who has risked and given everything to the search for divine truth.

As fears of an environmental apocalypse grow, and the terrible dangers that afflict humanity on every level become more and more inescapably clear, Rumi's work will become increasingly important for its testimony to the divine origin and purpose of human life, its overwhelmingly beautiful celebration of the truths and mysteries of Divine Glory, and its wise embrace of all paths and approaches to the experience of God. Increasingly, it will become clear that Rumi is not only humanity's supreme mystical poet but also one of its clearest guides to the mystical renaissance that is trying to be born in the rubble of our suicidal civilization. What might be called the "Return of Rumi" to the consciousness of humanity occurs at a time when the truths of Rumi's celebration of the Beloved are needed not only as revelations of the real purpose of human life but as essential inspirations and empowerments in the struggle to save the human race and preserve the planet. Unless the vision of Rumi and other great mystics from the major traditions possesses the spirit and hones the motivation of millions of human beings and initiates them into the sacredness of human life and the holiness of Nature, humanity will destroy the world in a bitter frenzy of ignorance, pride, and greed.

If Rumi is to be given, as I believe, a central role in the awakening of humanity to its own divine truth and possibility, then it has never been more important to see his work and the teaching it enshrines in as lucid and fearless a way as possible. The New Age in its narcissism, its lazy greed of appropriation, its ability to make over all sublime and demanding truth in its own hazy image, and its lack of any real or ennobling concern for political, social, and environmental issues, has created a limited vision of Rumi to serve its own ends; has created, in fact, what I call "Rosebud Rumi," a Californian hippie-like figure of vague ecstatic sweetness and diffused "warm-hearted" brotherhood, a kind of medieval Jerry Garcia of the Sacred Heart.

This limp and vulgar vision entirely omits an essential side of Rumi's spiritual genius—its rigorous, even ferocious, austerity. Rumi is indeed an ecstatic, the greatest of all celebrators of that ecstasy that streams from the Presence of Love. He is also—as I hope this volume will make clear—the canniest, shrewdest, most unsentimental, and sober of teachers, very un-New Age in his refusal to deny the power of evil, his candor about the limits of all worldly and earthly enlightenment, his Jesus-like suspicion of all forms of wealth and power, and his embrace of the sometimes terrible and prolonged suffering that authentic transformation must and does demand. This rigorous, fierce, authoritative Rumi, the veteran of the wars of Love, is what our spiritual renaissance deeply needs to listen to and learn from, if the transformation that is trying to happen in our time is not to be diffused in a cloud of laziness, fantasy, denial, and occult charlatanry.

Rumi can be a complete guide for seekers now precisely because he combined the most extreme imaginable vision and experience of divine beauty and mystery with a sober and humble teaching of how to sustain, continually deepen, and integrate them with daily life. Unlike many of our contemporary teachers, drunk on partial awakening, Rumi— whose knowledge of the Path of Love was perhaps the most thorough that any human has ever had—never claimed total enlightenment; in fact, one of his most original contributions to the history of mystical thought is his intuition that evolution is an infinite process that never ends on any of the planes of any world, and that the journey into embodying and living Love is as infinite and boundless as Love Itself. Unlike many contemporary seekers, Rumi's passion was not for sensational experiences, occult powers, or radically enhanced "self-esteem"; he was dragged deep enough into Love to know that divine life could only be found on the other side of an Annihilation of self that demanded and cost everything and that authentic spiritual "Lordship" was not the acquisition of any kind of power but a humble embrace of "Servanthood"—of the life of the servant-slave of Love and so of every human and sentient being in the name, and for the glory of, God. Such a vision is simultaneously far more humble and more exalted than the pseudo-mysticisms being peddled everywhere in the New Age, and sometimes in Rumi's name. The laws of such a final vision of human truth and divine possibility are not tailored as are so many of the contemporary mystical "systems," either to flatter human weakness or to inflate human claims to divinity; complete experience gave Rumi an unfailing sense of balance and a fundamental and astonished humility before the always changing and always deepening experience of the Divine.

This balance and humility inform Rumi's teaching at every level and are the source of its extreme clarity about the dangers, temptations, fantasies, and various forms of inflation, hysteria, and pride that threaten the authentic seeker. They are also the source of perhaps its most challenging, even frightening aspect—that of Rumi's fearless and scathingly truthful embrace of the ordeals that true transformation demand. Rumi's own awakening was at the price of a vast suffering, or rather, series of sufferings, that led to his death and rebirth in the dimension of Resurrection. Rumi knew from bitter and glorious experience, that the life of the real lover of God is often one of frightful ordeal and exposure to bewilderment and grief of every kind. Yet, because Rumi both lived and survived such appalling experience, he is able to speak with ennobling courage and hope about the gnosis that is born from it and about the glory of sustained divine human being that Annihilation opens onto, the inner "Rose garden" that only a pure-souled dying-into-Love can uncover in all its amazing rapture and loveliness.

All authentic seekers will, if they are sincere, come by

Divine Grace to the test of the Cross, of the Great Death in which the false self and all its fantasies and games are systematically destroyed to reveal the presence of the Divine and deathless Self within. In this time of ordeal, when everything depends on a capacity for sustained adoration, blind, half-mad faith, and the ability to expose the heart again and again to radiant and sometimes murderous danger, Rumi's work will provide the most luminous guidance and a clear and holy encouragement to ever-deeper surrender. Such encouragement is especially important in a time like ours when the entire planet and nature itself are passing through an experience of prolonged breakdown, even crucifixion. More than ever we need guides to ordeal and its hidden mystical meanings, and Rumi, of all mystics and teachers, is the most experienced in what might be called the "alchemy of agony." The splendor of his fearlessness, humility, and endless courage can help us all develop those powers of insight and trust that could enable us to transmute catastrophe into an opening for massive spiritual growth.

The Teachings of Rumi is divided into four different "movements" and is conceived as a rich interconnected "symphony" of mystical instruction. The four movements follow the development, as Rumi understood it, of the journey of the soul to its Origin and of the transmutation of the lover into the Beloved. The first movement, "The Call," is dedicated to the beauties, glories, trials, and demands of the first stage of the Path, the stage of Awakening, and to the necessary commitments to prayer and spiritual discipline that alone can deepen its truth in the seeker's being. In the second movement, "Be a Lover," the reader is taken into the shrine-room of the Heart, where the supreme secrets of Love and its working on the whole being of the Lover are given and celebrated and where Rumi's championing of the primacy of the way of longing and passion is opened up in its wisdom and power. The third movement, "Ordeal," explores the nature, meaning, price, and demand of the sustained ordeals that always follow on a fervent abandon to Divine Love and that prepare the lover for the Great Death, the Annihilation-in-Love, that must occur for the passing-over into Resurrection and Unity-Consciousness to be possible. In the last movement of this mystical symphony, "Union," the wonders, ecstasies, and endless evolutionary possibilities that Union opens up to the seeker are celebrated from many different angles. In Union, the Journey to God has become the Journey in God; Rumi makes it clear that such a journey has no end in any dimension, and that its mysteries are finally beyond the reach of any human expression or even understanding. The movement ends with a series of Rumi's holiest meditations on death, on the mystery of inner relationships beyond time and space, and, most especially, on the relationship between the humble loving reader and the work and guidance that stream—and keep streaming—from Rumi's own deathless consciousness. By this time, I hope it will be clear to the sensitive reader that what he or she is receiving through the medium of Rumi's words is a timeless transmission from the Heart of the Beloved Himself, a transmission whose holy accuracy and effectiveness can only expand as the seeker's own experience, courage, and gnosis ripen and fructify.

I have taken the different quotations of *The Teachings of*

Rumi from the whole range of Rumi's work. I have used and juxtaposed odes, letters, and table talk, stories about Rumi's own transforming presence from his biographer Aflaki, and sections from the *Mathnawi*, his vast mystical epic, and I have interwoven prose and poetry and story in a way that I trust will constantly challenge and enliven the reader. Ideally, I would like the reader to experience the book as the turning of a vast diamond of gnosis, of which each "teaching" is a "facet" in which all the others can also be seen glittering.

I have worked to render the passages from Rumi as accurately but also as transparently as possible and to make them always accessible to a modern reader. On rare occasions, I have cut and slightly changed where I thought appropriate. I have worked from the original, with the help of scholar friends, and a plethora of translations in many languages, most notably those of A. J. Arberry, R. V. Nicholson, and E. H.Whinfield. The most profound influence on me has been that of Eva de Vitray Meyerovitch whose magisterial translations of over a thousand odes and the complete *Mathnawi* into French have been my constant companions for years and a model for me of rigor, dignity, and availability.

May the testimony of Rumi to the glory and power of Love humble, illumine, and embolden us all! May all of us know on earth and in a body the saving mysteries of our divine identity and enact them in the Real in works of justice and compassion to help transform and preserve our planet!

Nevada, August 15, 1998

PART I

The Call

"Go on a journey from self to Self, my friend . . .
Such a journey transforms the earth into a mine of gold."

MATHNAWI

The Wine and the Cup

THE WINE of divine grace is limitless:
All limits come only from the faults of the cup.
Moonlight floods the whole sky from horizon to horizon;
How much it can fill your room depends on its windows.
Grant a great dignity, my friend, to the cup of your life;
Love has designed it to hold His eternal wine.

MATHNAWI

You Are the Macrocosm

You MAY seem to be the microcosm;
In fact, you are the macrocosm.
The branch might seem like the fruit's origin:
In fact, the branch exists because of the fruit.
Would the gardener have planted the tree at all
Without a desire and hope for fruit?
That's why the tree is really born from the fruit
Even if it seems the fruit is created by the tree.
The idea which comes first comes last in realization—
Particularly that idea which is eternal.

MATHNAWI

Our Soul Was Like the Universe

BEFORE "GARDENER" or "vine" or "grape" existed in this
  world
Our soul was drunk with the Eternal Wine.
We proclaimed "I am the Supreme Reality"
In the Baghdad of the spiritual world
Before Al-Hallaj's's condemnation and death on the gibbet.
Before the universal soul became the world's architect
Our life was happy in the wine shop of Divine Realities.
Our soul was like the universe, our soul's cup like the sun.
The universe was drowned in the light of the soul's wine.

MATHNAWI

Return at Last

How LONG will you move backwards? Come forward!
Don't stray towards disbelief, come to religion.
In grief see gentleness: come towards gentleness.
Return at last to the origin of your own origin.
Although you may seem to be the child of earth
You are the Son of the pearls of certainty,
The faithful guardian of the treasure of Divine Light:
Return at last to the origin of your own origin.
When you have tied yourself to detachment from yourself
Know you'll be sprung free of your "I"
And escape that prison with its thousand traps.
Return at last to the origin of your own origin.
You're of the race of Adam, the Caliph of God,
But you've lowered your eyes to this bad world,
And satisfied yourself with meager scraps.
Return at last to the origin of your own origin.
Although this world has you still in its thrall
In your heart, you're a hidden treasure.
Open now your inner eyes, the eyes of Love:
Return at last to the origin of your own origin.

ODES

The Goal Is One

THE PATHS are many, but the goal is one. Don't you see how many roads there are to the Kaaba? For some the road starts from Rome, for others from Syria, from Persia, or China; some come by sea from India and the Yemen. If you are considering the different roads, the variety is immense and the difference infinite; if you consider the goal, however, they are all in harmony and are one. The hearts of each and every one of them are fixed upon the Kaaba. Each heart has one overriding attachment—a passionate love for the Kaaba —and in that there is no room for contradiction.

That attachment to the Kaaba cannot be called either "impiety" or "faith": it is not mingled with the various paths we have mentioned. Once the travelers arrive at the Kaaba, all quarreling and vicious squabbling about the different paths—this person saying to that "You're wrong! You're a blasphemer!" and the other shouting back in kind—simply vanish; they realize that what they were fighting about was the roads only, and that their goal was one.

TABLE TALK

One Light, Different Windows

THE PROPHETS are like one single being. If you refuse one of them, you refuse them all.

It's like ritual washing. If you don't wash one of your organs and wash all the others, it will be of no use. So, as the prophets recognize each other, if you don't admit one of them, it is as if you had admitted none of them. In fact, there's only One Light that appears through different windows and which reaches us through the person of each prophet. All of these lights stream from the same Sun.

If you refuse a part of this light, that shows that you're a bat. You're like a bat who says, "I am against this year's sun, but I accept last year's." In fact, this year's and last year's sun are not different in any way. Whatever difference you think you perceive comes from the fact that you didn't really experience last year's sun.

LETTERS

The Authentic Human Being

THE HUMAN BEING who can do without God and makes no effort to realize God is not a human being at all; while if he were able to understand God, then that would not be God. The authentic human being, then, is one who is never free from striving, who turns restlessly and endlessly about the light of the Majesty of God. God is He who consumes man and makes him nothing, since no reason can understand Him.

TABLE TALK

Rumi and the Ox

ONE DAY, our Master went to visit the tomb of his father Beha-ed-din Weled. By chance, the town butchers had bought an ox to sacrifice it; all at once, the animal broke its rope and escaped from them; everyone started to run after it but couldn't either follow or capture it. On its path, the ox met Rumi; immediately, it stopped, went shyly towards him, and seemed by its attitude to beg forgiveness of him. Our Master caressed the ox with his holy hand; the butchers—who by now had caught up—asked to have the ox back. "Do not kill this ox," the Master said. "Set it free." The butchers obeyed him; the ox took the country road out of town.

After a while, the friends arrived. Rumi told them, "An animal that was being prepared for slaughter escaped and came to us. God—may He be exalted always—has saved him from death. If a human being, with all his soul and heart, turns his face towards God, God will deliver him from the Flayers of Hell and make him attain Paradise; there is nothing astonishing in that." It is said that no one saw the ox afterwards: it disappeared in the countryside of Konya.

AFLAKI

The Moon Is the Same Moon

Know that the world of created things
Is like pure and limpid water
In which shine the attributes
Of the Omnipotent One.
Consciousness, justice, mercy
Are like stars of heaven
Reflected in the running water.
Kings are the theater
Of the royalty of God;
Sages are the mirrors
Of God's Eternal Wisdom.
Generations have passed away,
A new generation has come;
The moon is the same moon
But the water's not the same.
Justice is the same justice,
Knowledge the same knowledge,
But generation has replaced generation
In a long and endless chain.
Generation after generation
Have gone into the dark
But the Divine Attributes
Are changeless and eternal.
The water in this river

Has changed innumerable times;
The reflection of the moon and stars
Has remained unaltered.
Its origin is not the water
But the Light-Kingdoms of Heaven.

MATHNAWI

You Yourself Become Illusion

I KNOW this world; it never fulfills its promises.
You won't find a real friend in the whole world.
Don't go on gazing at that gilded disk in the sky:
It has nothing inside it, not even a straw mat!
So many idiots swarm into the trap of this world
Like blind men who don't have a stick to hand!
They worry for this world and tremble at its poverty.
Bizarre lunacy which nothing can ever cure!
It's easy to credit the world's beauty since it stays veiled.
In reality, it's a hideous old hag, without any allure.
Whoever submits to her witchcraft is like a serpent
Without feet, or hands, or intelligence, or religion.
What an absurd fate to give your life to this world!
It's the fate of all those who don't find the path to Him.
What is this copper full of dross, that forgets its copper-
    nature
And imagines that the philosopher's stone doesn't exist?
Because of a vain image, you yourself become illusion
And then all you can know is grief, anguish, and disaster.

MATHNAWI

The Elephant, the Candle, and the Eye of the Sea

SOME INDIANS took an elephant into a dark house to exhibit it. People entered the house to try and find out what it was like, but since it was too dark for them to see anything clearly, they each had to feel the elephant with their hands. One person put his hand on its trunk and said, "This animal is like a water-pipe!" The hand of another brushed its large ear; it seemed to him like a fan. Another seized its leg and declared, "The form of the elephant is like a pillar!" Another put his hand on his back and proclaimed, "The elephant is like a throne!"

Each time anyone heard a description of the elephant, he would understand it through the particular part he had touched. According to whichever section of the animal they had encountered, people's affirmations differed. If each of them had held out a candle in the dark all differences between what they said would have vanished.

The eye of outward sense is only like the palm of a hand; how can you discover an elephant in its totality with just a palm? The eye of the sea is one thing, the foam another; leave the foam aside, see with the eye of the sea.

MATHNAWI

Don't Listen to the Trickster

THE CARNAL SOUL'S food is seeds of evil—
Sow them, and they grow and grow irresistibly.
The cow cannot sing like the nightingale:
Lucid intelligence knows nothing of the taste of
    drunkenness.
The wolf cannot breed the beauty of Joseph's face:
The peacock could never lay a serpent's eggs.
Don't you see the carnal soul has stolen every life
And mirrors for you a theater of false tomorrows?
The whole of life is now, is today, is this eternal moment.
Never listen, promise me, to the promises of this trickster.
Untie the knot of existence and reign in your fantasies
So you can at last escape the tyrannical false self.
You say you long for musk? Then find the plain
Where the gazelles of Tartary roam and feed.

ODES

A Quarrel about Grapes

A MAN GAVE a coin to four different people. One of them, a Persian, said, "I want to buy some *'anghur'* with that!" The second man was an Arab and he said, "I want *'inab'* not *'anghur,'* you worthless fool!" The third was a Turk and he said, "This is my money and I don't want *'inab.'* I want *'uzum.'* The fourth, a Greek, shouted, "Shut up all of you! I want *'israfil!'*"

In their madness, the four started to argue and hit each other because they didn't know the hidden meaning of names. They battered each other with their fists because they were empty of true knowledge and filled with ignorance.

If an authentic mystic master, proficient in many languages, had been there, they would have been pacified. He would have said, "I can give you everything you want with this one coin; if you give me your heart sincerely and without dissimulation, this coin will accomplish all you want. Your one coin will become four; four enemies will become one heart. All you say only produces struggle and separation; what I tell you brings harmony. So be quiet now, so I can talk for you."

MATHNAWI

Lift Now the Lid of the Jar of Heaven

Pour, CUPBEARER, the wine of the invisible,
The name and sign of what has no sign!
Pour it abundantly, it is you who enrich the soul;
Make the soul drunk, and give it wings!
Come again, always-fresh one, and teach
All our cupbearers their sacred art!
Be a spring jetting from a heart of stone!
Break the pitcher of soul and body!
Make joyful all lovers of wine!
Foment a restlessness in the heart
Of the one who thinks only of bread!
Bread's a mason of the body's prison,
Wine a rain for the garden of the soul.
I've tied the ends of the earth together,
Lift now the lid of the jar of heaven.
Close those eyes that see only faults,
Open those that contemplate the invisible
So no mosques or temples or idols remain,
So "this" or "that" is drowned in His fire.

ODES

The Three Pearls

When God created the pure body of Adam he drew it out of the earth and breathed into it His sacred breath and said to Gabriel, "Take from the sea of My Omnipotence three pearls, place them on a plate of light, and present them to Adam so he can choose one." The three pearls were reason, faith, and humility.

Gabriel presented the plate to Adam and told him what God wanted. Adam, illumined by the divine light, chose the pearl of reason. Gabriel wanted to take back the plate with the two pearls it still held to the sea of Omnipotence; but, because of their heaviness, he did not have the strength to lift them. The pearls of faith and humility then said to him, "We cannot separate ourselves from the holy company of our friend Reason; without him, we cannot establish ourselves firmly or even exist. During ancient times we were all three the jewels of the mine of Divine Glory; the pearls of the Sea of Omnipotence are inseparable."

Then the voice of God rang out, "Gabriel, leave the two pearls where they are and return!" So Reason installed itself at the peak of the human intellect; faith lodged itself in Adam's pure and sensitive heart; humility reigned on his holy face.

These three pure pearls are the heritage of the children of Adam. Every child descended from Adam who is not adorned by these pearls and does not shine with their brilliance is shut off from the Light and deprived of authentic gnosis.

AFLAKI

The Thicker the Veil, the More Valuable the Jewel

People claim that there exists in the human soul a kind of depravity you do not find in animals or wild beasts. Since men do not practice surrender and obedience to God they become inferior to the animals. God has said in the Koran of people like these: "They are real wild animals, and even more lost."

Bad character and depravity in man are a veil that hides his deep essence; these dark dispositions see to it that his essence is veiled, and this veil cannot be dissolved except through immense efforts. These efforts are of every kind. The greatest is to mingle with friends who have turned their face towards God and have turned away from this world. There is no combat harder for a human being than to associate himself with holy and pious people: seeing them annihilates and dissolves the carnal soul. They say, "When a serpent hasn't seen a man for forty years, it becomes a dragon; it becomes this because it hasn't met or seen that being that could be the cause of the dissolution of its perversity or of its evil character."

Wherever a strong lock is used, there is something extremely precious hidden. The thicker the veil, the more valuable the jewel. A hoard of treasure is guarded by a large snake; don't dwell on the hideousness of the snake, contemplate the dazzling and priceless things you'll discover in the treasure.

Aflaki

Become the Sun Itself

A TRUE SEEKER must transcend those joys and delights that are just the ray and reflection of the glory of God. He must not let himself grow content with such things, even though they are of God, come from God's grace, and are of the radiance of God's beauty, for they are not eternal; with reference to God they are eternal: with reference to man, they are not.

Think of the rays of the sun shining into houses. They *are* rays of the sun, and they *are* light, but they are attached to the sun and not the houses. When the sun sets, their light no more remains.

What we have to do, then, is to *become* the Sun itself, so all fear of separation can forever be ended.

LETTERS

The Real Pilgrimage Is Inward

Y OU WENT ON pilgrimage to Mecca, but where are
  you now?
Come, come; here is where you find the Beloved.
Your Beloved's your nearest neighbor, just a wall divides
  you:
What idea possessed you to wander through the desert?
If you see the form without form of the Beloved
You're at once the Lord, the House, and the Kaaba.
You've entered the house ten times the same way:
Now, just once, leave it, and climb onto the roof.
The House of God is beautiful, you've described it
  completely:
Now show us a sign of the Lord of the House.
You say you've visited the garden, where are your roses?
You're coming out of the sea, you say, where's the pearl of
  your soul?
May so many stark ordeals be transmuted into treasure!
Alas, it's you yourself who hide your own treasure.

MATHNAWI

The Thirsty Man, the Wall, and the Water

On THE BANK of a stream there was a high wall
And on top of the wall a sad and thirsty man.
The wall prevented him from reaching the water
That he longed for passionately, like a fish.
Suddenly, he threw a brick into the water—
The sound of the water struck his ears like words
Spoken by a delicious and tender friend. . . .
Because he was so happy hearing the water,
He began to tear down the wall and throw brick after brick.
The sound of the water seemed to be saying,
"What do you think you gain by doing this?"
The thirsty man replied, "I gain two things
And will never stop doing what I'm doing.
The first is that I hear the sound of the water
Which is like an oboe to a thirsty man.
This sound's for me like the Angel of death's trumpet—
It awakens life in one who was dead!—
Or like the drum of thunder during the days of spring
That makes the garden bloom in all its glory,
Or like the days of almsgiving for a beggar,
Or the news of his freeing for a prisoner.
The second gain I get from doing what I do
Is that with every brick I tear down and throw

I come closer to the running water.
Every brick I take down makes the wall lower—
Lowering the wall is a way of reaching the water.
Destroying the wall's separation leads to Union."
Tearing off the carefully linked bricks is Prostration—
Didn't God announce, "Prostrate and approach Me?"
As long as the wall stands, it's an obstacle
To the one who bends his head in prayer:
You'll never completely prostrate to the Living Water
While you're not sprung free from the physical body.
The thirstier the man on the top of the wall is,
The quicker he tears down the bricks and tufts of grass.
The more in love with the sound of the water,
The greater are the clumps of brick he tears down.

MATHNAWI

False Thinking

Infinite mercy flows continually
But you're asleep and can't see it.
The sleeper's robe goes on drinking river water
While he frantically hunts mirages in dreams
And runs continually here and there shouting,
"There'll be water further on, I know!"
It's this false thinking that blocks him
From the path that leads to himself.
By always saying, "Further on!"
He's become estranged from "here":
Because of a false fantasy
He's driven from reality.

MATHNAWI

The Paradox

I WILL HUNT for the Beloved with all my power
And all my strength and passion until I know
It is futile to look for Him.
Yet how could I know His Presence near me
Without traveling across the world?
How could I grasp Its sublime Mystery
Without risking a long journey?
God has told us He is with us
But has sealed the heart
So it cannot understand this
Except slowly and indirectly.
When you have accomplished many journeys
And fulfilled the Path's duties,
The seal will then be withdrawn from your heart.
Then you'll say to yourself, "If I'd known
I was always so extremely near to God
How would I have been able to look for Him?"
Yet this knowledge depended on a journey:
Sharpness of mind alone could never win it.

MATHNAWI

The Place of Honor

MANY SAGES and sheikhs at an assembly were discussing where the place of honor was. Sheikh Siradj-ed-din claimed, for example, that "In the colleges of scholars, the place of honor is in the middle of the sofa where the professor sits." Sheikh Cadr-ed-din said, "According to the mystics, this honor is given to the side of the sofa where the shoes are left."

After this, as a kind of test, the question was posed to our Master. He replied:

"Where are the threshold and place of honor? The place where our Friend is found. The place of honor is where the Friend is."

"And where is he?" asked the Seyyid Cheref-ed-din.

Rumi replied, "Are you blind? Don't you see Him? Haven't you eyes to look at Him? From your head right down to your feet is Him, entirely Him."

Rumi stood up immediately. Dancing began and grew more and more impassioned. All the dignitaries present tore their robes in ecstasy.

AFLAKI

Busy Yourself with That Head

IT IS THE TIME of Union, of Vision, the time of
    Resurrection and Eternity.
It is the time of grace and generosity, the sea of perfect
    purity.
The treasure of gifts has arrived, the shining of the sea has
    flashed out.
The dawn of blessing has arisen. Do I say dawn? No, the
    Light of God.
What is this "figure," this "face"? Who is this "Emperor"
    and "Prince"?
What is this "ancient knowledge"? All these are only veils—
Only ecstasies like this one can transport you beyond them.
The source of such live waters is in your head, and in your
    eyes:
Busy yourself with that head—yet, in reality, you have two!
Your clay head comes from earth, your pure head from
    heaven.
How many pure heads have rolled in the bloody dust
So you can know that it is on *that* head that this depends!
Your original head's hidden, your derived one's manifest:
Behind this world opens an infinite universe.

ODES

Taste with Discrimination

For the carnal soul, there are wines of damnation
That make the slave of desire stagger from the true Path.
For the spiritual intellect, there are wines of such divine
   happiness.
It wins the house that no one could want to leave,
And by its drunkenness uproots the tent of heaven
And takes the path that soars free of all earthly direction.
Don't be deceived, my heart, by every kind of drunkenness;
Jesus is drunk on the Beloved, the donkey on oats.
Look for holy wine like this in the jars; one's full of dregs
Another—and this is the one you need—pure as pearls.
O connoisseur of wine, take care, taste with discrimination
So you find a wine that hasn't been adulterated.
Both jars will make you drunk, but holy drunkenness
Will take you to the Lord of Judgment and free you
From all thought, all anxiety, all desperate expedients,
While your inspired reason goes forward without obstacles
At the careful and measured pace of a camel.

MATHNAWI

You Are Loved by Him

If, in the school of Divine Love
You don't even know the alphabet
Don't worry; you'll be filled like Mohammed
With the Light of Reason.
Don't worry if you're not famous;
God knows best and hides his servants
Like a treasure, for their security
And in places that are little known.
Would you put your treasure
Where any fool could discover it?
The Love of God is a fire
That consumes all difficulties:
Daylight chases away all ghosts.
You are loved by Him; look for the reply
In the same place the question came from.
The cornerless corner of the heart
Is the royal road to God:
The radiance that is neither East nor West
Comes from a single moon.
Why do you go on, O mountain of Reality,
Hunting your echo here and everywhere?
Look for the reply in the same place
You bent in adoration towards
When broken by grief you kept repeating,

"O my God, O my God, O my God!"
Sell intelligence and talent and buy pure wonder:
Hurry towards humility, not Bokhara!

MATHNAWI

Leave the Vulture Behind

DISCURSIVE REASON'S a vulture, my poor friend:
Its wings beat above a decaying corpse.
The Saint's Reason is like the wings of Gabriel:
It soars in splendor, from stage to stage,
To rest in the shade of the Tree of Heaven.
It says, "I'm a royal hawk, I'm glorious and abundant,
I've nothing to do with a corpse, I'm not a vulture—
Leave the vulture behind and let me be your guide.
Just one of my wings will be of more help to you
Than a hundred thousand vultures in full flight."

MATHNAWI

Such a Passion and Longing

T HERE IS in the core of man such a passion and longing that even if he owned a hundred thousand worlds, he would never find peace. Look at how people dabble in every conceivable trade and craft; they study astronomy and medicine and all kinds of other things, and never find peace, for they have not obtained the object of their search. And what is that? It is the Beloved and the Beloved alone that is called "Heart's Ease." Where else but in the Beloved could the heart find ease?

All other joys and pursuits are like a ladder. You cannot stay on any of the rungs of a ladder; the really happy person is the one who is vigilant and understands this. The Path then becomes short for him, and he doesn't waste his entire life on one or another of the ladder's steps.

TABLE TALK

The Heart's the Only Real House of Safety

Rejoice in Him and nothing else but Him:
He is Spring; all other things are winter.
Everything other than Him drags you slowly to damnation,
Even if it's your throne and kingdom and crown.
Rejoice in grief; grief's the way to melt into Him;
Ascension, on this path, travels from heights to depths.
Grief's a final treasure and suffering a mine:
But how could mere children understand this?
When children hear the word "game," they start to run
With the carefree noise and speed of wild donkeys.
Blind donkeys! Go that way, you'll find only traps:
Run that way, you'll find massacres waiting.
Arrows fly, but the bow is hidden: From that hidden world
A hundred arrows of white hair fly to kill your youth.
Set out now, while you're strong, on the heart's vast plain:
You'll never discover joy on the plain of the body.
The heart's the only house of safety, my friends:
It has fountains, and rose gardens within rose gardens.
Turn to the heart and go forward, travelers of the night;
There's where you'll find trees and streams of Living Water.

ODES

Keep Your Heart Awake

THERE ARE many whose eyes are awake
And whose hearts are asleep;
Yet, what can be seen
By mere creatures of water and clay?
But he who keeps his heart awake
Will know and live this mystery;
While the eyes of his head may sleep
His heart will open hundreds of eyes.
If your heart isn't yet illumined
Be awake always, be a seeker of the heart,
Be at war continually with your carnal soul.
But if your heart is already awakened,
Sleep peacefully, sleep in the arms of Love,
For your spiritual eye is not absent
From the seven heavens and seven directions.

MATHNAWI

Measuring out the Sugar

Wisdom is like the rain. Its source is limitless, but it comes down according to the season. Grocers put sugar in a bag; their supply of sugar, however, is not limited to what's in the bag. When you come to a grocer, he has an abundant supply of sugar. But he sees how much money you have brought with you and measures out the sugar accordingly.

Your money on the Path of God is courage and faith, and you will be taught according to your courage and your faith. When you come looking for sugar, your bag will be examined to see how much it can hold; it will be filled accordingly.

Table Talk

Nearness Is of Many Kinds

Nᴇᴀʀɴᴇꜱꜱ ᴛᴏ Gᴏᴅ is common to us all,
Because we're all created and sustained by God,
But only the authentically noble
Possess and live that nearness
That's a constant upswelling passion of love.
Nearness is of many kinds, my friend;
The sun shines at once on mountains and gold,
But between sun and gold there's an affinity
The trembling willow knows nothing about.
Dry branches, as well as green, are near to the sun;
How could its blazing be concealed by either one?
Green branches, from their nearness, bear ripe fruit;
The dry branch grows only more desiccated.
Don't be drunk like the dry branch
Which, when it grows sober, is covered with regret;
Be one of those drunkards
Who make intellectuals blanch with envy;
Their whole being is alight
With the holy dancing flames of the Wine.

Mᴀᴛʜɴᴀᴡɪ

Keep Moving, Keep Growing

IF A TREE could uproot itself from one place to another
It would never need to fear the saw, or any blows of
    bad luck.
Neither the sun nor the moon could lavish their light
If they stayed motionless as a rock.
How bitter the Euphrates and Tigris would be
If they stayed in one place like the sea!
The air that stagnates in a pit becomes poisonous;
Look how the air sickens because of its inertia!
When the water of the sea travels towards the clouds
It frees itself from bitterness and acquires tender power.
When a fire stays without shooting out flames
It transforms itself to ashes, dead and destroyed.
Look how Joseph of Canaan, after leaving his father,
Went into Egypt and became famous forever.
See how Jesus, son of Mary, in his continual wanderings
Became the Water of Life and made the dead rise.
I have shown you a few signs; now, learn the rest yourself:
Accomplish the journey beyond yourself and reach God.

ODES

Make Yourself Ready to Do All He Wants

THE WORD of the Prophet, "Whatever God wills will
    happen,"
Doesn't at all mean be lazy and leave everything to Him.
What the Prophet wants is to inspire you to work and
    devotion.
What He means is "Make yourself ready to do all He
    wants."
When you're told that whatever Allah wills will happen
And that to Him belongs eternal, absolute authority,
Why don't you turn around Him like a slave
With the will and passion of a hundred men
To pay Him homage and shower Him with devotion?
If you were told the Sultan wanted this and that
And that his was the final, omnipotent authority,
Wouldn't you run to serve him with a hundred men's
    strength
So he could lavish on you benefits and gifts?
You wouldn't run away from him and his palace—
That wouldn't be the way to secure his help.
Turn around the Lord, then, since He has all the power
And kills His enemies and saves and sustains His friends.
Everything He wants, you'll certainly come to obtain;
Don't stray from Him, choose to honor and serve Him.

Don't do it because you're afraid to be rejected and
    damned—
Real lovers serve ardently, hopefully, in an ecstasy of awe.

MATHNAWI

On the Limits of Fatalism

You have feet—why make out you are lame?
You have hands—why then hide your fingers?
When a master puts a spade in a servant's hand
He doesn't need words to make his meaning clear.
Our hands, like that spade, are signs of God;
Understand the signs He flashes into your heart
And give your life to be in harmony with them.
He'll give you hint after hint about the mysteries;
He'll remove your burden and give you authority.
Are you carrying His burden? He'll give you the strength.
Are you receiving His order? He'll grace you His grace.
Accept His Order and you'll become His witness:
Look for Union with God and you'll become one with Him.
Your free will's your effort to thank God for His gifts;
Fatalism's a negation of all these gifts.
Giving thanks for the power to act increases your power;
Fatalism takes this gift out of your hands.
Fatalism is like sleeping on the journey; don't sleep!
Don't sleep before seeing the door of the threshold!
Fatalism is sleeping in the middle of thieves—
Can a cock who crows too soon expect peace?
If you really trust in God, then work hard,
Sow the seed, and lean on the Almighty's help;

Struggle as long as you can in the way of the Prophets.
Effort isn't a war with destiny:
Destiny itself has imposed on us this effort.

MATHNAWI

Another Alchemy

Sheikh Bedr-ed-din of Tabriz, the architect of the celebrated tomb in that city, was unique in his era in his skill in alchemy and in many different occult sciences. All day he would dutifully attend the companions in their resolutions; all night he would occupy himself in alchemical operations, through which he was able to procure pieces of silver and gold for the friends.

One day Rumi entered into his lonely laboratory and saw him plunged in work. The sheikh was so terrified at the Master's sudden appearance he couldn't move. Rumi took the anvil Bedr-ed-din had been using into his own hands and gave it back to him; the sheikh saw that it had changed into gold and shone with divine light.

Rumi then said, "If you must make gold, make this kind of gold; it is a process you won't need any apparatus or weaver's combs or anvils for. If you go on giving your whole strength to the work you are pursuing now, then when death comes, all you will leave behind you is a reputation of a master forger; when your gold reverts to brass, all the repentance in the world will be of no use. So, devote all your energies so that the brass of your own existence can become gold, and your gold can become pearls; what these pearls are cannot be described in any language."

Then Rumi recited:

Jesus will change your brass into gold
And if there is already gold in you, Jesus will make
  pearls from it.
And if there are pearls within you, Jesus will make
  them
Even more beautiful than the Moon or Jupiter.

At once Bedr-ed-din tore his clothes and gave up his art.

AFLAKI

On Repentance

Disbelief transforms gold into bronze, and peace
  into war.
Its falsity engenders a negative transformation:
It changes fertile earth into stone and pebbles.
It isn't given to every heart to prostrate in prayer:
The pledges of divine mercy aren't given to every servant.
Take care! Don't commit crimes and sins saying to yourself,
"I will repent tomorrow and take refuge in God."
Real repentance requires tears and fire in the heart!
Lightning and clouds are its indispensable condition.
You need fire and water for the fruit to ripen:
How can that occur without lightning and clouds?
Before the heart has shattered into lightning
And before rains of tears have fallen from your eyes,
How can the fire and menace of God's anger be appeased?
How could the green of the desire for Union grow?
How could the springs of limpid water start to flow?
How could the rosebuds whisper their secret to the garden?
How could the violet seal a pact with the jasmine?
How could the plane tree open its hands in prayer?

MATHNAWI

More Than One Stage Has to Be Transcended

Be always thankful, never be lured by vanity,
Don't be contemptuous, listen attentively, don't boast:
I am the slave of the one who never considers
He's attained the table of Union with God.
More than one stage has to be transcended,
So one day the traveler can arrive home.
Although the iron becomes red, it isn't so by nature;
Its redness comes from something that inflames it.
If the window of your house is full of light,
Don't think anything else luminous but the sun.
Each door and wall proclaim, "I am luminous!
I don't just reflect the light, I am it."
The sun laughs, "Idiots! Just wait until I set,
The truth of what you claim'll become obvious!"
Plants say, "We are green from our own power!
It's our nature to be joyful and green and high!"
Summer says to them, "Fools! Let's just see
How you'll all look when I leave!"
The body boasts of its beauty and elegance,
And the spirit which has hidden its wings and feathers
Says to it, "You dungheap, who do you think you are?
It's because of my shining you live a day or two.
You can make all the disdainful faces you want,

Just wait for what'll happen when I vanish!
Those whose love warmed you will dig your tomb
And make you a food for ants and reptiles.
Those who often came to you aflame with desire
Will stop up their noses at your stink."

MATHNAWI

See to It That You Pray Constantly

Rumi used to say again and again: "In the name of God, see to it that you pray constantly, so that your worldly means and heirs and friends become numerous; when the Resurrection comes, you will console your friends through these prayers. It is certain that, through the blessing that is attached to prayer, anyone who asks and begs will be granted their desires both on the Path and in the world."

It is also reported that when Rumi saw someone occupied assiduously in the accomplishment of the rites of canonical prayer, he would cry out: "Well done, servant full of zeal, humble and modest slave! That man is brave that cannot be shaken from the service of his master, and who practices his devotions for as long as he has the strength."

Aflaki

The Soul and the Spirit of Prayer

I HAVE TOLD you that prayer is a virtuous act. However, the soul and spirit of prayer are more virtuous than the form. Through them we arrive at Union with God, in a way that only God knows.

The condition of prayer, from an external point of view, is to be made ritually pure by water; the spirit of prayer is to make the heart bleed and weep tears of blood through a spiritual war of forty years, to be freed from seven hundred veils of shadows, to go beyond all those shadows and live from the life and existence of God.

LETTERS

The Pure Name

Praising God is pure; when purity has come
All filth packs its bags and leaves.
Contraries flee from contraries; night flies
When the light of dawn breaks.
When the Pure Name comes into your mouth
Neither impurity nor griefs remain.

Mathnawi

Your Longing for Me Was My Messenger to You

A LOVER WAS plunged in prayer when Satan appeared
  and said,
"How long are you going to go on crying, 'O Allah!'
 Shut up because you'll never get an answer."
 The lover was sad and hung his head in silence.
 Then, he had a vision of the Prophet Khidr who said,
"Why have you stopped calling on God?"
"Because the answer 'Here I am' did not come."
 Khidr said, "God Himself has ordered me to come to you
 And say, "Wasn't it I who commanded you to pray?
 Wasn't it I who made you busy with My Name?
 Your calling out, 'Allah, Allah!' was My 'Here I am!'
 Your longing for Me was My messenger to you:
 Of all your tears and cries and supplications,
 I was the magnet and it was I who gave them wings."

MATHNAWI

All through the Night God Is Calling Us

Don't sleep for just one night, my beautiful friend,
And the treasure of Eternity will appear before you.
The Sun of the Invisible will warm you all night;
The collyrium of mystery will open your eyes.
This evening I beg you, fight against yourself, don't sleep
So you discover those splendors that spread ecstasy.
It is at night that beauties unveil themselves;
The one who sleeps never hears their soft calls.
Wasn't it at night that Moses saw the burning bush
And heard its miraculous summons to come closer?
It was during the night he traveled so far
That he came to see a bush drowned in glory.
The day's for earning a living, the night's for love
So the eyes of the jealous cannot spy on you.
The rest of the world may sleep; but real lovers
Throughout the night talk inwardly with God. . . .
All through the night God is calling us,
"Rise up, use this time richly, you poor man!
If you don't, you'll burn with regret
When your soul's separated from your body."

Odes

Moses and the Shepherd

Moses saw a shepherd walking up and down and
   praying,
"O God, who chooses whomever You want—
Who are You, so I can become Your servant
And sew Your shoes and comb Your hair?
O that I could wash Your clothes, and kill Your lice,
And bring You milk, O my Beloved!
O that I could kiss Your little hands
And rub Your little feet, and when You go to bed,
Sweep and clean Your little chamber!
I offer You my goats in sacrifice!
Thinking of You makes me groan out loud!"
The shepherd was saying crazy things like these.
Moses cried out; "Who do you think you're talking to?"
The shepherd replied, "To Him who has created us,
By whom the earth and sky are made visible."
"Watch out!" thundered Moses, "You've become twisted!
You're a blasphemer now, not a Muslim.
What's all this rubbish! Stuff up your mouth with cotton!
The stink of your blasphemy has filled the world
And shredded the silk robe of religion!
Shoes and stockings might be fine for you
But how could they be useful to the Sun?
If you don't stop saying such things

A fire'll fall from heaven and burn the world.
Some of it's come already, otherwise why
Would there be so much smoke in what you say?
Why else would your soul now be so black
And your spirit be rejected by God?
If you really know that God's the Judge
How could you have found your crazy talk just?
The friendship of a fool is enmity:
God in His greatness doesn't need such service.
Who are you talking to? Your paternal and maternal uncles?
Does the Lord of Majesty have a body and bodily needs?
Only someone who develops and grows drinks milk;
Only someone who needs feet puts on shoes—
And if your words are addressed to His servant
To one whom God has described as "He is me and I
    am He,"
Then they're just as mad and blasphemous.
Speaking without any respect to the elect of God
Murders the spirit and blackens your whole life. . . ."
The shepherd cried, "Moses, what you've said has
    silenced me,
And burnt my soul to ash with repentance."
He tore his clothes, sighed, turned hastily
Towards the desert and vanished into it.
A revelation then came to Moses from God:
"You have separated my servant from Me.
Have you come to unite or to divide?
As far as you can, don't make a step towards separation;
The most hateful of all things to me is divorce.
I have graced everyone their way of acting:
I have given to everyone their own form of expression.

When another worships in his way it merits praise;
If you imitated him, it'd be worthy of blame.
For him, his adoration's honey; for you, it's poison.
I am independent of all purity and impurity,
Of all laziness and all diligence in worship.
I haven't ordered my worship to profit from it,
But to bestow a benefit upon My servants.
For Indians, the language of India's admirable;
For the people of Sind, the language of Sind.
I am not sanctified by their glorification:
It is they who become sanctified and pure.
I do not consider the tongue and its words;
I look at the spirit and character.
I look into the heart to see if it's evil;
The heart's the essence, words only the accident:
The accident's accessory, the essence is what matters.
How many more phrases, ideas, metaphors, can I stand?
It's burning I want, true burning! Become burning's friend!
Fire your soul with the passion of adoration:
Destroy with this fire all thought and expression.
Moses, those who know conventions are of one kind—
Those whose souls and spirits burn are another."
For lovers, love's flame arises with each moment:
Taxes and tithes aren't for a village in ruin.
If a lover speaks faultily, don't call him at fault;
If he bathes in blood, don't go and wash the martyr—
Blood, for martyrs, is preferable to water—
Their impurity's worth more than a hundred holy works.
In the Kaaba's interior, there's no *qibla* to turn to—
What does it matter if the diver has no shoes?
Don't look for directions to those who are drunk;

Why order those whose robes are in tatters to mend them?
The religion of love's different from all other religions;
For lovers, God is their religion and their faith.

MATHNAWI

True Consciousness

Tʀᴜᴇ ᴄᴏɴsᴄɪᴏᴜsɴᴇss has two wings, opinion only one:
Opinion is riddled with faults and its flight is short.
A bird with just one wing will fall flat on its face;
Even if it fights to get up, it'll fly only a few yards.
The bird of opinion, rising and falling like this continually,
Is only using one wing in its attempt to fly home.
When this bird has been freed from opinion, however,
Consciousness will show it its face and the bird of one wing
Will be graced with two and stretch them out grandly.
It will walk straight and strongly, without
Falling on its face ever or falling sick.
It will take flight then, with two wings, like Gabriel,
Without opinion or uncertainty or any discussion.
If the entire world said to it, "You are in God's path
And you are following the authentic religion,"
Such praise would not augment its fervor in any way,
For its solitary soul associates with nothing worldly.
And if everyone were to say to the bird, "You're lost!
You think you're a mountain; really, you're only a straw,"
It wouldn't fall into doubt because of such reproaches
And wouldn't be afflicted if everyone abandoned it.

Mᴀᴛʜɴᴀᴡɪ

The Sublime Art of Gathering-in

IF IN WINTER, trees do not put out leaves and bear fruit, does that mean they are idle? Of course not! They are always at work. Winter is the season of gathering-in, summer the season of giving. Everyone sees the giving, but not the gathering-in.

A man decides to give an extravagant feast and spends vast sums of money on it. Everyone sees the feast and its splendor, but no one sees or knows anything of the months or years of gathering in resources of all kinds that preceded it. That gathering-in, however, is the root of the whole business. Without an income how could there be anything to spend?

In the mystical life, gathering-in is prayer and silent contemplation, adoration, and thanksgiving: giving is the performing of acts of love and justice in the world. Breathe in through worship the majestic peace, bliss, and strength of the Most High; breathe out in loving and just action the power that has been bestowed on you by the Beloved.

TABLE TALK

Draw Strength from Reality through Form

ONE DAY the Prophet was asked, "Although the highest truths are always hidden, is it possible to derive strength from them through the mediation of form?" The Prophet replied, "Of course. Look at the form of heaven and earth!"

Draw strength from Universal reality through the medium of form; contemplate the turning of the wheel of the sky, the rain falling from the clouds in the right season, summer and autumn and winter and all the transformations of time. Don't you see that all these things are happening in an orderly manner and in harmony with wisdom? Does the mindless cloud *know* it is necessary to rain in the right season? Does the earth consciously have any idea how it receives seed and makes it flower tenfold in harvest? "Someone" *does* this; gaze on that "someone" through the mediation of this world and grow serene and strong.

TABLE TALK

Find a Home in the Heights

If you can detach yourself from all worldly worries,
You will live in the rapture of Eternity's garden.
If you purify yourself with the holy water of abstinence,
The murkiness of your heart will change into clear light.
If you can separate yourself from the house of desires,
You will come into the sanctuary of Divine Majesty.
In the heart of the ocean of Unity, you're not
A pearl that any worldly money can buy;
If you're brave enough not to grovel in the dust,
You can find a home in the heights of heaven.
If you dive now headfirst into profound contemplation,
You can dissolve all the past debts of destiny.
Doing such things are the sign of the real seeker—
The signs of fire of those who race along the Path.

Mathnawi

Be Worthy of My Gifts

THE QUEEN OF SHEBA sent a gift of forty horse-loads of gold to Solomon. When she came to Solomon's country, however, she saw that the mountains and fields, and even the dust on the roads, were all pure gold. Day after day she rode on gold until gold lost all meaning or value for her.

When Solomon saw her gift, he laughed out loud. "I never asked for—or wanted—gifts of any kind. All I ask from you is to be worthy of the gifts I'll give you."

TABLE TALK

The Man of God

THE MAN of God is drunk without wine.
The man of God is full without bread.
The man of God is distraught and astounded.
The man of God neither eats nor sleeps.
The man of God is a king under his robe.
The man of God is a treasure in the ruins.
The man of God isn't made of air and earth.
The man of God isn't made of fire and water.
The man of God is an ocean without limits.
The man of God makes pearls rain without clouds.
The man of God possesses a hundred moons and heavens.
The man of God possesses a hundred dancing suns.
The man of God is made wise by Supreme Truth.
The man of God isn't instructed by books.
The man of God is beyond faith or godlessness.
For the man of God just and unjust are alike.
The man of God has ridden out of nonbeing.
The man of God is served with dignity.
The man of God is hidden, O Shams-od-din!
Friend, go look for the man of God and find him!

ODES

Become a Fool

Since intelligence goads you into vanity and pride
Become a fool so your heart stays pure—
Not a fool, of course, who lowers himself to stupid jokes,
But one who's lost and astounded in Him.
The fools I am speaking of are like the Egyptian women
Who cut their hands when they saw Joseph;
They were stupid in what concerned their hands,
But wise for they saw perfectly Joseph's beauty.
Sacrifice your reason for love of the Friend;
All reasons spring from the place where He lives.
Those who are spiritually awake have always
Dispatched their reason to live in His district;
Only the mean-souled go on living where He doesn't.
If, through wonder, your reason leaps out of your head,
Each of your hairs will become a new head and reason.
Then, the pain of incessant thought will not crush your
    brain
For there "brain" and "reason" produce fields and orchards
    of gnosis.
If you turn to those fields, their subtle speech will reach
    you;
If you come to those orchards, your palm tree will break
    into flower.

Mathnawi

Resurrection

THE ONLY condition for experiencing Resurrection
Is to die first; what does Resurrection—*ba' 'th*—mean
   after all?
It means: "Making the dead come back to life."
The entire world has taken the wrong direction;
Everyone's in flight from nonexistence
When it's the only lasting asylum.
How can we win authentic awareness?
By renouncing knowledge.
How can we seek salvation?
By renouncing personal salvation.
How can we look for existence?
By renouncing our existence.
How can we seek true spiritual fruit?
By not stretching out our hands
For the fruit of this Illusion.

MATHNAWI

PART II

Be a Lover

"The beloved is all that lives: the lover a dead thing."

ODES

A Life without Love Isn't a Life

IF DESTINY comes to help you,
Love will come to meet you.
A life without love isn't a life—
God doesn't take it into account.
Every second that unravels far from love
Is a source of shame before the Lord.
When you leave this house at last,
You'll only be able to carry what weighs nothing.
Time that passes in the torment of love
Will reveal itself tender as the patience of a father,
And the poverty you are ashamed of now
Will be for you an honor in the other world.
Although the bitterness of patience is suffocating,
It'll become in the end a wonder of joy.
When the lion of the spirit escapes his cage,
He'll run towards the fields of Splendor;
And when he descends from this donkey's carcass,
The King of the heart will be a king of rapture.
Only spread out the hem of the robe of effort—
A rain of gold will pour from heaven.
Whoever doesn't show himself humble today,

Will tomorrow be humiliated like Pharoah.
Whoever isn't transformed like the rose into rosewater
Will be cast like thorns into the fire.

ODES

Not the Garden but the Gardener

ONE DAY Rumi's wife, Kira-Khatoun, asked him about the mysterious meaning hidden in the *hadith*: "Most of the inhabitants of Paradise are imbeciles." Rumi replied, "If they hadn't been imbeciles, how could they have been satisfied merely by paradise and its streams?"

To explain further what he meant, Rumi recited these verses:

> If, in hell, I could touch the curls of Your hair,
> I'd be ashamed of the state of the elect in heaven.
> If, without You, I was called to the fields of heaven,
> That vast space would be too narrow for my heart."

Rumi then said, "Every low-souled person who confines himself to contemplating the garden remains deprived of the vision of the Gardener." He added this marvelous verse:

> For me, Paradise without Him is Hell and the Enemy;
> I have been burnt by that terrible splendor
> That is the Glory of the Lights of Eternity.

AFLAKI

See the Friend Directly

THERE'S NO CURE, except the retreat into love,
For the suffering of subtly afflicted hearts.
See the Friend directly, or burn in longing for Him—
What does the whole world matter, apart from that?
To arrive, at last, at the vision of the Friend,
Keep your soul prostrate before the image you have of Him.
Stay standing before Him like the foot of a lamp;
A thousand graces are poured out to the noble.
In this contingent universe, you are powerless;
When will you find the origin of time?
When physical vision has transcended space,
Another sky opens to the eyes of the soul.
Your body is a saucepan, the soul its food.
Place this pan on the fire of divine passion
So its flames can make boil the truth within you.
Then you won't need anyone else's poems or teachings—
You yourself will know the value of your state of soul.

MATHNAWI

Love Is All That Exists

Be drunk on love, because love is all that exists;
Without love, no one has the right to enter His house.
They ask, "What is love?" Reply: "Giving up your self-will."
He who hasn't given up his will isn't chosen.
The lover's an emperor, the two worlds are at his feet:
Does an emperor notice what is thrown in his path?
It is Love and the Lover that live eternally—
Don't lend your heart to anything else; all else is borrowed.
How long will you go on and on embracing a corpse?
Embrace the soul that is embraced by nothing else.

Mathnawi

The Soul of Reality

How marvelous a lover is, for he gathers power, grows, and fills with vibrant energy from the image of his Beloved. This should not surprise you; think of how much perpetual strength the image of Layla fed Majnun.

Since the image of what is after all a transient beloved possesses so great a power to embolden the lover, why are you surprised that the Image of the Eternal Beloved should stream strength into the Lover, both here in this world and in the Invisible? That Image is not "Imagination" at all; it is the Soul of Reality.

TABLE TALK

The Root of the Entire Matter

Abu Bakr was not considered superior to you because of a great deal of praying, fasting, and giving of alms, but because of something that was fixed in his heart. The Prophet says that Abu Bakr's superiority over others was not because of prayer and fasting continually, but because God's special grace was with him in the form of his love for God. On the Day of Resurrection, men's prayings and fastings and giving of alms will all be put in the Balance: when love is brought, however, it will not be able to be contained in the balance. So the root of the entire matter is love.

So when you feel love hot within you, feed it with the fire of longing so it can burn hotter. And when you feel the goal of all things—the Quest for God—to be alive in you, feed that search by passionately searching further and deeper for "in movement is blessing." What is not increased, diminishes. Are you any less than earth? Men change it by turning it over with their spades, and it yields crops. When they don't turn it over, the earth hardens. So when you see the passion for the Quest is vibrant within you, keep that passion fiery.

TABLE TALK

Through Love

Through love bitter things seem sweet.
Through love scraps of copper are turned to gold.
Through love dregs taste like clear wine.
Through love agonies are healing balms.
Through love thorns become roses.
Through love vinegar becomes rich wine.
Through love the scaffold becomes a throne.
Through love disaster becomes good fortune.
Through love a prison becomes a rose garden.
Through love burning fire is a fragrant light.
Through love the devil becomes an angel.
Through love stones become soft as butter.
Through love grief is like delight.
Through love demons become servants of God.
Through love stings are like honey.
Through love lions are harmless as mice.
Through love sickness is health.
Through love the dead are resurrected.
Through love the emperor becomes a slave.

ODES

Only Love Can Explain Love

BEING A LOVER shows itself in pain of heart;
No evil is comparable to this pain in the heart.
The suffering of lovers is different from all others;
Love is the astrolabe of the mysteries of God.
Whether love comes from earth or from heaven,
In the end it draws us to the Beloved:
Whatever I say to explain or describe Love
When I arrive at Love itself, I'm ashamed of my words.
The commentary of words can make things clear—
But Love without words has more clarity.
My pen was rushing to write its thoughts down;
When it came to Love, it broke in two.
In speaking of Love, the intellect is impotent,
Like a donkey trapped in a bog:
Only Love itself can explain Love,
Only Love can explain the destiny of lovers.
The proof of the sun is the sun itself:
If you want proof, don't turn your face away.

MATHNAWI

The Beloved Is Everything

ONLY THAT BEING whose robe's torn by great passion
Is purified of greed and all its harm!
Blessing on you, Love, who bring us your gifts,
Who is the doctor for all our evils,
The cure for our pride and vanity, our Plato and Galen!
Through Love, our earthly body has flown to heaven,
The mountain began to dance and became agile.
Love inspired Mount Sinai, O lover! So Sinai
Grew drunk and Moses fell down, stricken with glory.
I also, like a pipe, can say anything at all
When I'm joined, in harmony, with my Friend:
Separate from the one who speaks, I grow silent,
Even if I know a hundred songs.
When the rose has gone and the garden faded,
You won't hear any more of the nightingale's story.
The Beloved is all that lives, the lover a dead thing.

ODES

Secret Ways

Kɪɴɢ, ꜱᴀɪɴᴛ, thief, madman—
Love has grabbed everyone by the neck
And drags us to God by secret ways. . . .
How could I ever have guessed
That God, too, desired us?

Oᴅᴇꜱ

Astounding Comfort

THE PERWANE asked Rumi, "When the servant of God performs an action, do the grace and good flow from the action, or are they the gift of God?"

The Master answered, "It is the gift of God and his grace. Yet God, out of His tenderness, ascribes both to the servant saying to him, 'Both are yours.' No one knows what astounding comfort is laid up for them in secret, as a reward for doing Love's work."

AFLAKI

Love, the Black Lion

Love has robbed me of sleep; that is what Love does.
Love doesn't give a fig for "soul" or "reason."
Love's like a black lion, famished and ferocious,
Who only drinks the blood of the heart of lovers.
Love seizes you tenderly and drags you towards the trap:
When you fall in, he watches you from afar.
Love's a tyrannical prince, a pitiless judge:
He tortures and oppresses the innocents.
Fall into his hands and you'll weep like clouds,
Run from him, and you'll freeze over like snow.
Each second he shatters a thousand cups in pieces;
In one moment he sews and tears apart a hundred robes.
He makes thousands of eyes weep, and that makes him
    laugh.
He slaughters a thousand beings and thinks of them as one.
No one can escape his chains by trickery or madness;
No sage can wriggle out of his nets by wisdom.

MATHNAWI

Let Yourself Be Killed by Him

THIS LOVE sacrifices all wise and awakened souls,
Cuts off their heads without a sword, hangs them without
    a scaffold.
We are the guests of the One who devours His guests,
The friends of the One who slaughters His friends.
When He sees a Joseph, He tears him apart like a wolf;
When He sees a believer, He slits his throat like a
    blasphemer.
We have offered Him our hearts, either to be consoled
Or, if killed, killed with humanity and mercy.
No, His breath gives back life to the one He's killed,
Although by His gaze He brings death to so many lovers!
Let yourself be killed by Him, is He not the water of life?
Don't grow bitter, for the Friend kills with tenderness.
Keep your soul noble, for this noble love
Kills only kings near God and men free from all earthly ties.
We are like the night, earth's shadow: He is the Sun;
He splits open the night with a sword soaked in dawn.

ODES

My Heart Is "Light Upon Light"

I<small>F A HUNDRED BEINGS</small> like me are annihilated, what does
  it matter?
He won't have any fewer lovers with wounded hearts!
He said to me, "Why are your eyes so fixed on My face?"
Because my eyes wet with tears look for the heat of the
  sun.
Like Ishmael, I offer myself to the wound of His knife;
It is Abraham I want, although he intends to kill me.
If my passion's notorious, God knows I have an excuse,
I am slave to a love that has a million drums and standards.
The grief He causes me is like a treasure in my heart.
My heart is "Light upon Light,"
Like the beautiful Mary who carries Jesus in her womb.

O<small>DES</small>

Lover and Love Are Only One

W<small>HAT FEAR</small> should a real lover have of the Path
Since the Eternal Himself is his companion?
What grief could he feel at the soul's departure
When the God of his soul is his closest friend?
He's a traveler; yet, like the moon,
He stays immovable in his own beauty.
How could he wait for the coming of the breeze
Who is himself lighter than any breeze?
Lover and love, my soul, are only one:
Never think that they're two halves.
When love and lover have become one,
Both are at once the Giver and the Gift.
The lover is in search of this fullness;
He is like leather laid out in the maturing sun.
When he goes to the sea in search of the pearl,
He is himself a pearl, a unique, priceless pearl.

O<small>DES</small>

Rose Garden after Rose Garden

Lovers know there are roses
In the bloody veil of Love;
They live astounded
By Love's matchless beauty.
The intellect says,
"The six directions are blocked!"
Love says, "There's a way!
I've taken it thousands of times."
Intellect sees a market
And starts to haggle;
Love sees thousands of markets
Beyond that market.
How many mystic martyrs
Hidden in Love's soul
Have abandoned the preacher's chair
To climb onto the scaffold!
Lovers who drink the wine's dregs
Reel from bliss to bliss;
Dark-hearted skeptics
Burn inwardly with denial.
Intellect says, "Stay where you are!
Annihilation has only thorns!"
Love laughs, "The thorns are in you!"
Keep silent, and tear Being's thorn

Out of your heart;
Discover in your own soul
Rose garden after rose garden.

O D E S

Love's Intelligences

In SUBLIME and radiant Love you'll find intelligible things
Very different from the things intelligible here.
To God belongs intelligences other than yours
By which all heavenly things and powers are ruled.
With your individual intelligence you procure the things to
    live:
With your universal intelligence—and through Love's
    mercy—
You make of the planes of heaven a carpet under your feet.
When you sacrifice your intelligence for love of the Lord
He'll give you it back tenfold, or seven hundred fold.
When the women of Egypt sacrificed their intelligence
They ran toward Joseph's pavilion of Love.
Love, the cupbearer, withdrew their minds from them—
And they drank their fill of wisdom for their whole lives.

MATHNAWI

Look for Passion, Passion, Passion, Passion

Passion burns down every branch of exhaustion;
Passion's the Supreme Elixir and renews all things;
No one can grow exhausted when passion is born!
Don't sigh heavily, your brow bleak with boredom;
Look for passion, passion, passion, passion!
Futile solutions deceive the force of passion;
They're bandits who extort money through lies.
Marshy and stagnant water's no cure for thirst
However limpid and delicious it might look;
It'll only trap you and stop your looking for fresh rivers
That could feed and make flourish a hundred gardens—
Just as each piece of false gold prevents you
From recognizing real gold and where to find it.
False gold will only cut your feet and bind your wings,
Saying, "I will remove your difficulties," when, in fact,
It is only dregs, and defeat in the robes of victory.
Run, my friends, run far away from all false solutions!
Let Divine passion triumph and rebirth you in yourself!

MATHNAWI

Love Makes the Seas Boil
Like a Pot

To Majnun, who loved Leila with total passion,
The wisdom of this world
Wasn't worth a blade of grass.
Dirt and gold were equal in his eyes;
Why even mention gold?
For Majnun, his life itself was valueless.
Lions and wolves and wild beasts knew him
And swarmed around him like his family,
Knowing he was purified of all animality
And filled with divine passion
And that his skin and fat would be poison for them.
The sweetness spread by Heavenly Reason
Is poison to the wild animal
And if the animal eats it, even metaphorically,
The lover's flesh will become poison and kill him.
Everything, in fact, except Love is devoured by Love.
For Love's vast beak, the two worlds
Are nothing but a single grain of wheat.
Does a grain ever turn and eat the bird?
Does his feeding trough ever stand up
And turn to devour a horse?
Serve God, if you want to be a lover.
Service is a way of winning love, and it works.

The servant of God longs to be sprung free of destiny;
The lover of God never hungers for freedom.
The servant wants a robe of honor for his trouble;
All the robe of honor the lover desires
Is the vision of the Beloved.
Love is not contained in speaking or hearing;
Love is an ocean whose depth is invisible.
There are innumerable drops in this boundless Sea;
The seven seas are nothing to this Ocean.
Love makes the seas boil like a pot,
And rubbles the mountains to sand,
And splits the heavens into fragments,
And makes tremble the entire earth.

MATHNAWI

It Itself Becomes Sign

THE ONE to whom's unveiled the mystery of love
Exists no longer, but is annihilated in love.
Place before the sun a burning candle,
See how its shining disappears before those lights:
The candle exists no longer, is transfigured into Light.
There are no more signs of it; it itself becomes a Sign.

ODES

Joy Will Unveil Itself

At breakfast, a lover asked her lover, as a test:
"Whom do you love more? Me or yourself?"
He replied, "I'm so annihilated in you,
I'm filled with you from head to foot.
Nothing's left of my own life but my name:
The rest is you. I'm dissolved like vinegar
In your ocean of burning honey,
I'm like a stone transformed into a ruby,
I've been filled with the sun's glory."
The stone's nature doesn't stay the same:
It becomes, entirely, filled with sun.
Then, if it loves itself, it's really
Loving the sun that is itself;
And if it loves the sun with all its soul,
It's loving itself that is the sun.
Whether it loves itself or the sun
There's really no difference at all;
Both loves are the rising Sun's radiance.
But until the stone becomes the ruby,
It's its own severest enemy
Because there's no one "I," there are two;
The stone's still dark and blind to the light
And since darkness wars against the light
If it loves itself then, it's a blasphemer,

Vehemently thwarting the sun's power.
That's why the stone must never say "I":
Untransformed, it is shadows and death.
Pharoah said, "I am God," and was utterly destroyed:
Mansur-Al-Hallaj said, "I am God," and was saved.
The first "I" calls down God's final fury;
The second wins the glory of Divine mercy.
Pharoah was a black stone and Al-Hallaj a diamond;
The first was the Light's enemy, the second its lover.
Al-Hallaj's "I" became "He" in his heart's vast depths
Through Union with the Light, not the doctrine of
    Incarnation.
Compel yourself to wear away your stone nature
So your stone can radiate the qualities of the ruby:
Show constancy in self-discipline and spiritual combat,
Contemplate eternal life ceaselessly while dying to
    yourself.
If you do, your stone's hardness will soften every moment
And your ruby nature will keep growing and being
    strengthened.
The characteristics of existence will drain from your body
And ecstasy's qualities increase in your spirit.
Become all hearing, become an ear, so you can
Obtain from Grace a brilliant ruby earring.
Be a true seeker, dig in your earth like a well maker,
Dig incessantly in the earth of your body
So at last you can reach the Living Water.
If the Inspiration of God arrives, even before your well's
    dug,
Live waters will spring in fountains from your soul.
Go on working constantly, don't attend to anything else;

Never stop clearing the earth for your well, little by little.
To all those who undergo ordeals, great treasures are
    unveiled:
Whoever tries with all his heart arrives at good fortune.
Didn't the Prophet say that praying and prostrating to God
Are knocking at God's door with the door knocker of Being?
Go on and on knocking with this knocker, my friend;
Joy will unveil itself to you and fling open the door.

MATHNAWI

PART III

Ordeal

"You want reality unmasked? Choose death!"

MATHNAWI

Destruction Precedes Renewal

A MAN STARTED to break up the earth with a spade.
A fool came and shouted at him, "Why are you ruining the
    soil?"
"You idiot!" the man cried. "Go away and don't bother me!
Understand the difference between destruction and
    growth.
How could this soil become a rose garden or wheat field
Before it's broken up and ruined and made ugly?
How could it become orchards and harvests and leaves
    and fruit
Before it is utterly destroyed and worn down?
Before you pierce an abscess with a knife
How can it heal and how can you regain your health?
Until the doctor purifies your humors with his cures
How can your illness disappear and true healing arrive?
When a tailor cuts up a cloth, piece by piece,
Does anyone go up to him and strike him and say,
"Why have you torn up this beautiful satin;
What can I do with scraps of torn-up cloth?"
Each time that builders come to repair an old building
Don't they begin by destroying what was there before?
Look at the carpenter or the blacksmith or the butcher;

With them too, you'll find destruction precedes renewal.
If you don't subject wheat to the grinding millstone
How will bread ever come to decorate your table?"

MATHNAWI

Enter the Furnace

Our MASTER spoke one day to a nobleman about mystical truth. He said, "In the state you have attained, you have become gold; now you must transform even more of yourself into gold; you have to come to a time when you will enter into the furnace, begin to boil, and offer yourself up for hammering on the anvil of mortification by the blows of the Coiner, so you can become a ring worthy of Solomon or an earring that could adorn an Emperor. Most of the seekers you see are just imitators; they will become authentic when they dare to enter the hearth of love, and when they endure on the anvil of patience the blows of misery and suffer impossible situations; then, after many ordeals, they will find purity, and become the mirror of God."

AFLAKI

The Mystery of Misery

ONE DAY, someone came to Rumi and started to complain of his poverty and bad luck. "Get out now," Rumi cried, "and from this moment on do not consider me a friend!"

Rumi then recited these noble verses:

Come, become like me, O face of the moon!
Don't look for fortune or the stuff of life—
If the devil had been as trusting
He'd have been the king and possessor of the standard.

Rumi added, "One day one of the companions of the Prophet said to him, 'I love you.' 'If that's so,' the Prophet replied, 'how do you stay standing? Put on your shield. Go forward to meet ordeal after ordeal, and be prepared for them, for misery is the gift He makes to those who love Him.' God said; 'Am I not your Lord?' and you replied, 'Yes, of course.' What is the mystery of this 'yes, of course'? To bear misery.'"

AFLAKI

Ordeals by Terror

THE PATH towards God is the sacrifice of self,
And in every thicket lurks a danger
Designed to make the person
Whose soul is fragile as a flask of glass
Turn back and retrace his steps.
The Path of religion is full of troubles and disaster
Because it is not a Path
Suited to anyone with a cowardly nature.
On this Path, the souls of beings
Are subjected to ordeals by terror
Like a sieve is used to strain the wheat.

MATHNAWI

The Work of Religion Is Astonishment

PHYSICAL SENSES are the ladder for this world;
Religious senses are the ladder for heaven.
Look for the health of the physical to a doctor
And for the health of the spiritual to the Beloved.
The health of the physical depends on a strong body;
The health of the soul ruins the body.
The Path ruins the body and after ruining it
Gives it back its full vigor and power.
It tears the house down to discover treasure
And then with the same treasure
Builds it back more beautiful than before.
It cuts off the water, cleans out the riverbed,
Then makes fresh drinking water flow through it.
It pierces the skin to take out the arrow shaft
And then new skin grows over the wound.
It razes the fortress to the ground and seizes it from the
    enemy
Then raises up a hundred towers and ramparts.
Who can describe the action of the Matchless One?
What I have said is only what I am allowed to.
Sometimes God's action is like this, sometimes quite
    different;
The work of religion is nothing but astonishment;

Not the kind that comes from turning your back on God
But the kind that comes from being wild with ecstasy,
From being drowned in God and drunk on the Beloved.

MATHNAWI

The Sign

Tʜɪs ɪs the sign you will obtain from God,
The kingdom and power you're looking for:
That you weep continually through the long nights,
That you're always ardent in your prayers at dawn,
That in the absence of what you're seeking,
Your day darkens and your neck becomes thin as a reed,
That you've given away all your possessions in alms,
So your goods are scattered like those who ruin all they
   have,
That you've given up what belongs to you, your sleep, your
   health,
That you've sacrificed your life and become thin as a hair,
That you've sat down—Oh how many times!—in the fire
   like an aloe branch,
That you've gone—Oh how many times!—like armor to
   meet the sword.

Mᴀᴛʜɴᴀᴡɪ

Look for the Happiness of a Supreme Lover

Before a flower can open in His rose garden
Thousands of thorns come to pierce it.
Although the soul has received only grief from Him,
Love has made her turn away from all worldly attachments:
She has preferred this anguish to all rewards.
She has chosen suffering above all joys.
In her eyes, His thorn is more glorious than any flower,
His lock more precious than all other keys,
His tyranny victorious over all earthly happiness.
The poison of His anger transforms itself into tenderness,
His refusal is worth far more than the agreement of others.
Cornelian and pearl are inferior to His stone.
Look for the happiness of a supreme lover of God—
All the joys of this world are nothing to it.

Odes

Grief Is Worth More Than the Empire of This World

God gave Pharoah hundreds of goods and riches,
So he laid claim to omnipotence and majesty.
During his entire life, this perverse man didn't feel
A single suffering that made him lament for God.
God graced Pharoah the empire of this world,
But he didn't grace him pain and suffering and ordeals.
Grief's worth more than the empire of this world
Because it makes you call on God in secret.
The cries of those free from pain are cold and dull:
The cries of the agonized spring from ecstasy.

MATHNAWI

Prudence

The Prophet said, "Prudence consists of staring evil in
   the face,"
Know, you madman, each of your steps is a trap.
The surface of the plain seems smooth and vast
But there's a trap at every step.
Don't go forward arrogantly.
The mountain goat skips along saying,
"I don't see any trap!"
While it races, the snare pierces its throat.
You who say, "Where is this trap?"
Look and gaze around you, and know
You've seen the plain but not the trap.
Without an ambush or lure or hunter
How come the sheep's tail's trapped in the wheat field?
All those who walked arrogantly on the earth—
Look at their skulls and bones.
When you go to the cemetery,
Ask their bones what happened
So you can see clearly those blind drunkards
Tumbled into the pit of illusion.
If you have eyes, don't walk blindly
And if you haven't, take a cane with you.
If you don't have the cane of prudence and judgment,
Take the eyes of one who sees as guide.

When you proceed, proceed like a blind man, so your feet
Avoid the ditch and the wild dogs.
The blind man makes his way trembling with fear,
Taking every precaution to avoid all nuisance.
If you don't act like him, you fool,
You'll have leapt far from the smoke
Only to fall headlong into the fire.

MATHNAWI

Keep Your Dragon in the Snow

A SELF-STYLED "dragon hunter" went into the mountains to trap a dragon. He searched all over the mountains and at last discovered the frozen body of an enormous dragon in a cave high up on one of the tallest peaks. The hunter brought the body to Baghdad. He claimed that he had slaughtered it single-handedly and exhibited it on the bank of the Euphrates.

Thousands of people turned out to see the dragon. The heat of the Baghdad sun started to warm up the dragon's frozen body, and it began to stir, slowly awakening from its winter hibernation. People screamed and stampeded, and many were killed. The hunter stood frozen in terror and the dragon devoured him in a single gulp.

> Your lower self is like that dragon, a savage tyrant.
> Never believe it's dead; it's only frozen.
> Always keep your dragon in the snow of self-discipline.
> Never carry it into the heat of the Baghdad sun.
> Let that dragon of yours stay always dormant.
> If it's freed it'll devour you in one gulp.

TABLE TALK

Give the Serpent a Kiss

"THERE'S NO COURAGE," the Prophet said, "before the
   battle has begun."
Drunkards vaunt their bravery when you speak of war
But in the blaze of battle they scatter like mice.
When it makes its plans, the heart's avid for wounds
But the first pinprick empties its sack of air.
I'm astonished by the man who says he wants purity
And yet trembles when the harshness of polishing begins.
Love's like a court case; to undergo fierce treatment
Is like a proof; no proof and you'll lose your case.
Don't be disturbed if the Judge demands proof:
Give the serpent a kiss to obtain the treasure.
This hardness is not directed at you, my son,
But at the many defects that hide within you.
When a man beats a carpet again and again with a stick,
It's not the carpet he's attacking, but the dirt in it.
If a man whips a horse, it isn't from rage or hatred—
He wants it to stop stumbling and go forward cleanly.
Unfermented wine is placed in a dark cold cellar
So after a while it can become real wine at last.

MATHNAWI

For Love, Like for a Furnace

My soul's a furnace; it's happy with fire.
It's enough for a furnace to be the house of fire.
For love, like for a furnace,
There's always something to burn—
If you don't see this,
You're not a furnace.

MATHNAWI

Offer Your Life to This Work

ABANDON ALL arrogance, all vanity, and acquire
  Majesty.
He said, "Am I not your Lord?" You replied, "Yes."
What is your reward? To pass through ordeals.
The secret of that "Yes" is to beat constantly
At the door of poverty and annihilation.
Purify yourself totally and become dust
So from your dust flowers can keep springing.
When you become a flower, dry, and burn joyfully
So from your burning Light may flame out.
If through your burning you turn yourself to ash,
Your ashes will become the philosopher's stone in the
  Invisible
Which birthed you from a handful of dust
And created the whole earth from the foam of the sea
And built all the heaven from black smoke!
This is the sacred stone that takes a piece of bread
And turns it into power for our whole life
And transmutes our vital breath into consciousness.
Offer your life to this work and this matter;
Poverty becomes lavish when it offers up its life.
You give up a life dark with every ordeal—
What do you receive? Happy, limitless existence!

ODES

A Supreme Grace

God has helped me understand a supreme grace—
The goodness hidden within cruelties,
The diamond beyond price hidden in dung.
The cruelty that comes from God
Is worth more than a hundred acts of mercy
From this world or any other.
To grow distant from God is torture to the soul.
God's worst cruelty is better
Than all the mercies of the two worlds.
How sublime the Lord of the two worlds is!
In His cruelty lives hidden tenderness:
To submit the soul to God out of love for Him
Makes its essential life blaze and grow.

MATHNAWI

Gaze in Wonder at the Infinite Rose Garden

CONTEMPLATE THE cupbearer, not the drunkard;
Look at Joseph, not your wounded hands.
You're a fish in the trap of the body;
Look at the fisherman, don't look at the net.
Contemplate the origin that was yours at the beginning,
Not this accessory that's yours only for a time.
Gaze in wonder at the infinite rose garden,
Don't consider that thorn that wounded your foot.
Contemplate the Bird of Heaven whose shadow shelters
    you,
Don't look at the crow that escaped your hands.
Like the cypress or ear of corn, grow towards the heights,
Don't, like the violet, always bow down to the ground.
In the stream of your being runs the Water of Life;
What does it matter to you if jar and jug are broken?
Put your trust in Him who gives life and Ecstasy;
Don't mourn what doesn't exist, cling to what does.

ODES

The Housewife and the Chickpea

Look at the chickpea in the pot, how it jumps
When it's put into the fire . . .
When you boil the water it's in, the chickpea
Leaps to the top of the pot and cries out,
"Why are you burning me? Wasn't it enough to buy me?
Why do you also have to afflict me?"
The housewife continues to push it down with her spoon,
"Be still and boil well! Don't jump far
From the one who makes the fire!
I don't boil you because I hate you:
I boil you to acquire taste and savor
So you can become food and mingle with life:
Your affliction doesn't come from being despised!
When you were fresh and green
You drank water in the garden:
You drank water then to prepare you for this fire."
The mercy of God precedes His affliction.
His Mercy has always preceded His anger
So you can obtain life's authentic wealth.
Chickpeas, you boil in trials and sufferings
So neither self nor existence may remain in you!
Become food, strength, and fine thoughts;
You were weak as milk; become a jungle lion!

Mathnawi

He Will Not Let You Die

You place your face against mine and whisper,
"Why has the King made me so thin and pale?"
He has set your barn of straw on fire
To grace you the alms of His own wheat,
And made you green as fresh grasses
To set you apart from the weeds of vanity.
In the furnace of Love, you're like Abraham:
Don't be afraid, He will not let you die.
Your intelligence has known the Night of Destiny;
Love is the portion Destiny reserves for you.
He's made you humble and flowing as a stream
To purify your being of all stains;
From every direction, agonies have crowded you
To drag you at last towards the Directionless.

MATHNAWI

Satan

In this vast prison of the world,
The food of true faith is rare;
By the tricks and games of Satan
What there is, is wasted.
Prayers, fasts, and ordeals
Might win us the food of devotion—
Satan will see that he eats it all.
Take refuge in God from His Satan!
Satan's disobedience has killed us!
He may be just one spirit
But Satan can enter a thousand beings
And everyone that Satan enters
Becomes a Satan like him.
Satan is in whoever freezes your passion—
The Demon is hidden under his skin.
When Satan doesn't find a physical form,
He'll invade your imagination
And make it drag you into evil:
From your thoughts His destruction will stream,
From thoughts even of peace or work,
Or the love of knowledge or of home and family—
No thought is safe from his twisting!
Take care! Say at once, "O God help me!"
Repeat it over and over again,

And not only with your tongue—
From the bottom of your soul.

MATHNAWI

You Have No Idea What You Are Asking For

ONE DAY Jesus was walking in the desert with a group of insincere and self-absorbed seekers. They begged him to tell them the secret name which he used to bring the dead back to life. Jesus said, "If I tell you, you will use its power wrongly." They swore they would use the knowledge humbly and wisely and went on begging him.

"You have no idea what you are asking for," Jesus said, but he told them nevertheless.

Soon afterwards, the group was walking in a part of the desert where the ground was heaped with whitening bones. "Let us see if the word works," they said, and they uttered it. Immediately, the bone heap clothed itself with flesh, transformed into a wild beast, and tore them to pieces.

TABLE TALK

Obstacles on the Path

THE WORLD of imagination and the illusion of fear and
  hope
Are great obstacles to the pilgrim on the path.
The images of this imagination were harmful
Even to someone like Abraham, who was as strong as a
  mountain.
Even he, that giant who threaded jewels of gnosis,
Was so seduced by the world of imagination and blinding
  illusion
That he said, "This is my Lord!" to a mere star.
If such an evolved and majestic being as Abraham
Can be so easily seduced away from the Path,
What will illusion not do to a goose or an ass?
Intelligences as strong as mountains have been drowned
In seas of imagination and whirlwinds of illusion.
If mountains, then, are beaten low by this Flood—
Where can you find any safety but in the Ark of Love?

MATHNAWI

One Small Hair

ONE DAY, giving mystical instruction, Rumi said:

"Just as in the Canon Law of the Prophet it is said 'There's a source of pollution hidden under every hair' and a person cannot be purified of his exterior pollution until every single hair of his body has been washed and not a single hair remains dirty, so, the true mystics tell us, as long as there remains in a person one single hair of his own personality, he cannot ever be purified of his own inner evil."

Rumi then said: "A man who had the qualities of a perfect saint took the road to Annihilation; suddenly, he soared beyond the Sea of Existence. One small hair of his personality, however, remained on him; in the eye of Absolute Poverty, this hair was as large as a girdle."

AFLAKI

The Tattoo Artist, the Lion, and the Man of Qazwin

A MAN OF Qazwin went to a barber and said to him, "Tattoo me and do it like an artist!" "O noble Lord," the tattooist said, "what shall I represent?" The man replied, "A furious lion. My ascendant is Leo. Fill your needles with blue."

The tattooist then said, "Where shall I begin?" The man replied, "On my shoulder blade." As soon as the tattooist began to work on him, however, pain invaded his shoulder and the man started to moan, "You're killing me! What image are you in the middle of designing?" "A lion," the tattooist replied, "just as you ordered." "Which limb of the lion have you begun with?" "The tail." "Leave the tail!" the man cried out. "My heart shivered from the blows of the needle."

The tattooist began to prick another part of the man's shoulder. "Which of the lion's limbs are you doing now?" "The ears." "Don't let the lion have ears," the man shouted. "Leave out the ears!" Again the tattooist began to work with his needle on another part of the shoulder blade. "What limb are you doing now?" the man screamed. "The stomach," said the tattooist. "Don't let the lion have a stomach! What does it need a stomach for?"

At this the tattooist was totally bewildered; he stood a

long time with his fingers in his mouth. Then, he threw his needle to the ground and said, "Am I dreaming or what? Who has ever seen a lion without tail or head or stomach? God himself never created a lion like that!"

> O my friend, bear the pain of the needle
> To escape the poison of your dark soul.
> Heaven, moon, and soul prostrate in adoration
> Before those who've escaped their own existence.

MATHNAWI

Peace after Long Exile

Eᴀᴄʜ ᴍᴏᴍᴇɴᴛ my new joy whispered in my ear,
"I will afflict you, but don't grow sad.
I will make you miserable and weeping,
To hide you from the eyes of the wicked.
I will make you bitter with grief,
So the Evil Eye will be swerved from your face.
You're not someone who can buy and possess me;
You're my slave prostrate before My Providence.
You hunt for tricks to be able to attain me:
You're as powerless to leave as to find Me;
In your grief you ache for a way to come to Me;
Last night, I heard your sighs fill the world.
Even in this waiting, I could, if I want,
Make you enter and show you the Path,
And free you from the whirlwind of time
And place your hands on the treasure of Union.
But the sweetness of the Place of Peace
Is proportionate to the pain of the journey.
You'll only enjoy the city and your relations
After enduring all the griefs and ordeals of exile."

Oᴅᴇs

Never Turn Away from Me

Gᴏᴅ ᴛᴀʟᴋᴇᴅ to Moses in the silence of the heart
And whispered, "O my chosen one, I love you!"
Moses answered, "O Generous One, tell me
Which part of my character makes You love me
So I can struggle to feed and embellish it."
"You're like a child," God said. "In its mother's presence,
Even if she pushes him away, he clings to her.
For him, there's no one else in the world—
All his agony and joy comes only from his mother:
If she slaps him, he still rushes and clings to her.
He doesn't look for help to anyone but his mother:
She is for him all evil and all good.
Your heart also, whether things are good or bad,
Never turns away from Me; in your eyes
All other beings are just stones and clumps of earth."

Mᴀᴛʜɴᴀᴡɪ

Despair Is a Sin

THE PROPHETS said, "Despair is a sin;
The grace and benefits of the Creator are infinite
You should never despair of such a Benefactor;
Hold on with all your strength to the stirrups of God."
Many miseries are hard to endure at the beginning
But then they are relieved, and their anguish vanishes.
After despair, many hopes flourish, just as after darkness
Thousands of suns open and start to shine.
Our duty is to resign ourselves and do what God wills.

MATHNAWI

Praise God and Be Patient

You're the Joseph of time and the sun of heaven!
Rise up from this ditch and prison and show your face!
Your Jonah's been afflicted in the belly of the whale:
There's no other way to set him free but praising God.
If Jonah had not praised God, the belly of the whale
Would have been his prison until the Day of Resurrection.
By glorifying God, constantly and fervently, he escaped.
What is glorification? The sign of the Day of Alast.
If you've forgotten the praise given to God by your spirit,
Listen to the praises of the saints and prophets;
Listen to the praises of those Fish of the Divine Sea.
Whoever has seen God is of God, that's certain:
Whoever has seen the Divine Sea is a fish.
This world's another kind of sea, this body another fish;
The spirit is Jonah cut off from the light of Dawn.
If you glorify God, you'll be delivered from this fish:
If not, you'll be eaten up, and vanish like smoke.
True spiritual Fish abound in the sea of this world;
You don't see them, although they fly around you.
These fish stream towards you; open your eyes and see
    them
And even if you don't succeed in seeing them clearly,
You will at least have heard them praising God.
Practicing patience is the soul of all praise:

Be patient, for that's the highest praise of God.
No other kind of glorification has so high a station;
Be patient; patience is the key to consolation.
Patience is like the bridge of Surat which souls after death
Must cross over to come at last into the Light of Heaven.
For each beautiful boy there's an ugly teacher;
Flee the ugly teacher and you'll never reach the boy:
The beautiful boy and the ugly teacher go together.

ODES

The Serpent

A WISE MAN was riding by at the moment when a serpent entered the mouth of a sleeping man. The horseman saw it, hurried to try to scare the serpent away, but it was too late. His vast intelligence revealed to him what he had to do: he gave the sleeper several fierce blows with a club, which made him wake up and run away and hide under a tree. Rotten apples from the tree lay on the ground; the horseman cried out, "Eat them at once!" and gave the man so many apples to eat that they tumbled out of his mouth.

"Why are you attacking me like this?" the unfortunate man kept howling. "What did I do to you? If you have a fatal grudge against me, strike me once with your sword and kill me! How terrible was the moment I came into your sight! Happy is the man who has never seen your face!"

Every time the man went on to pronounce a new curse, the horseman went on beating him, saying, "Keep running!" Blows rained down on the man and he ran and ran, sometimes falling on the ground. He was exhausted, worn out; his face and feet were covered with a thousand wounds. Until nightfall, the horseman made him run in all directions, until at last a vomiting possessed him, caused by bile from the apples he had eaten. Everything he had eaten, good or bad, spewed out of his mouth, including the serpent. When he saw the serpent leap out of his body, he fell to his knees before the holy man; his sufferings abandoned him the moment he grasped the full horror of the long black snake.

"How could I have known it?" he gasped to the horseman. "You are the Gabriel of Divine Mercy! I was dead; you gave me back life. You looked after me as mothers do their children. Happy is the man who sees your face or who appears suddenly before your house! Don't punish me for what I said; it was my madness speaking! If I had known anything of what you were up to, how could I have said such stupid words?"

The horseman replied, "If I had given you any idea of the danger you were in, you would have died of a heart attack; if I had described the characteristics of the snake, terror would have made you faint and die. Didn't Mohammed say, 'If I described openly the enemy in your souls, even the hearts of the brave would be shattered.' Shattered in this way, a person would not continue on his Path or bother about any work and in his heart neither perseverance in prayer would remain, nor any strength in his body for fasting and ritual prayer. He would become helpless like a mouse before a cat; he would grow crazed like a lamb stalked by a wolf. No power to complete his plans would remain in him. This is why I took care of you without saying anything. If I had spoken to you about the snake, you wouldn't have been able to eat what you had to, and so you wouldn't have been able to vomit it out. I heard your insults and continued doing what I had to do: I prayed continually under my breath, 'Lord save this man!' I did not have permission to speak of the reason for what I was doing, and it was not in my power to abandon you. Because of the grief in my heart, I said continually what the Prophet said at the battle of Ohod when he was wounded, 'Guide my people, Lord; they know nothing.'"

The man who had been saved from so much misery fell to his knees and cried out to the horseman, "You are my joy, my good luck, my treasure; God will reward you as you deserve! The poor being I am cannot know how to thank you. God will thank you, my guide: I do not have the power to do so."

I have told this parable to illustrate the "enmity" of the wise and to show that their "poison" is the satisfaction of the soul.

MATHNAWI

Now Die to Yourself

You've endured many terrible griefs
But you're still under a veil—
Because dying to yourself
Is the fundamental principle
And you haven't adhered to it.
Your suffering cannot end
Before this death is complete:
You cannot reach the roof
Before climbing up the whole ladder.
How could you ever experience
Your boat's total shipwreck
Before you've loaded it
With the final weight?
This final weight's essential;
It's a star that summons night
And it shipwrecks the boat of error.
When your boat of self-consciousness
Is finally broken and sunk,
It becomes like a sun
Flooding a cloudless sky.
Since you're not yet dead, however,
Your anguish goes on and on.
O candle of Taraz, die at dawn!
The sun of this universe is hidden

Until all the stars are hidden.
You cannot come to know God
But by denying what opposes Him.
You want Reality unmasked? Choose death!
Not the death that drags you to the tomb—
The death that is a transmutation
So you at last change into the Light.

Odes

My Work's to Risk My Head

I DON'T WANT any mercy, only the blows of the King;
I don't want any refuge but Him.
I have crumbled to nothing everything that's not Him;
Everything I am is consecrated to Him.
If He cuts off my head in His fury
The King'll grace me sixty other lives.
My work's to risk my head and forget myself:
His is to grace me a new head.

ODES

Heaven Is Made of the Smoke of Hearts

O MY GOD, be satisfied with your lovers!
May the death of lovers be holy!
May Your beauty be a feast for them!
May their souls burn like incense in Your fire!
O Beloved! You have spilled our blood with our own hand;
May that same hand also bloody our soul!
May anyone who says, "Save him from love!"
Have his prayer chased from heaven!
On the path of Love the moon dwindles and disappears.
May this dwindling, from love, become a fullness!
Others demand a respite from death
But lovers cry out, "No, let it come fast!"
Heaven is made of the smoke of hearts that burn away.
Praises to all those who are burnt away!

ODES

Do Not Despair, My Soul!

Do not despair, my soul! See, hope is arriving!
The hope of all souls has come from the Invisible.
Do not despair, although Mary is not here;
The light that took Jesus to heaven has come!
Do not despair, my soul, in the shadows of this prison
The King who ransomed Joseph from prison has come!
Jacob has left the tent where he was hiding;
Joseph who tore Zuleikla's veil has come.
You spent all night crying, "My Lord! My Lord!"
He who heard your "My Lord! My Lord" has come.
Your grief lasted so long! Look, healing is here:
Your door was locked, look, here is the key.
You mourned and fasted before the Table of Heaven:
Break your fast now, for the new moon is born.
Be silent, be silent, for by the command of God
The shock of amazement annihilates all words.

ODES

The Desert Where Love Appears

I HAVE COME to a desert where Love appears.
Everything impure there has found total purity.
What could coral be worth beside the price of the soul?
See how a sun appears to an atom!
There are thousands of locks, each vast as heaven—
A few letters in the shape of a key open them all.
My heart is like a vast tablet of light;
An ocean of agony drowned it again and again,
But it became a warrior, after being martyred a hundred
    times.
I venerate each one of the waves of this ocean:
I'm at once the feast and the disemboweled victim;
I'm the slave of a fish that comes from the sea.
Each drop of this sea clothes a form that appears:
Each form carries the name of a saint or mystic.
O my soul! Enter and purify yourself in this boundless
    ocean
Where one drop engenders a thousand graces and visions.
The swells and storms of Destiny imperil every ship
But in this Sea of Peace all find safety at last.

ODES

PART IV

Union

"Come, the rose garden has flowered!"

AFLAKI

Waters Constantly Flowing

THIS ENTIRE world's the form of Universal Reason,
Which is the Father of all lovers of the Divine Word.
Be ungrateful towards Him and nothing can change.
Make your peace with your Father, abandon disobedience,
And this world's water and clay will appear like a gold
    carpet
And Resurrection become your immediate experience
And heaven and earth be transfigured in your eyes.
Since I'm always at peace with my Father,
The world always appears like a paradise to me.
At each moment, a new form and new beauty appear
And their glory dissolves all fear and boredom.
I see the world radiant and brimming with magnificence;
The waters constantly flowing from the Springs of Heaven.
The sound of these waters is always enchanting my ears;
My deepest mind and consciousness reel with bliss.
The branches of the trees dance for me like penitents;
I see leaves everywhere clapping their hands like
    musicians.
The mirror's shining seeps through its velvet sheath—
Imagine the blaze when the Mirror itself appears!

ODES

Since You Are I,
You Who Are Myself

Once a man came and knocked at the door of his friend.
"Who are you?" asked his friend. "It is I," he replied.
The friend said, "Go away! This isn't the time to enter!
There's no place at a table like mine for the one
Who's not been cooked in the fire of true gnosis."
Apart from the fire of absence and separation
What'll cook the raw or free the uncooked from fraud?
The poor man went away and for a whole year of travel and
absence
He was burnt utterly by the flames of separation.
His heart burned until it was consumed; he came again
To the door of his friend and knocked at the door
With a hundred signs of the utmost fear and reverence,
Terrified a wrong word should escape his lips.
From within, his friend called out, "Who's at the door?"
He replied, "It is you who are at the door, O charmer of
hearts!"
"Since you are I," the friend said, "O you who are myself,
Enter; there's no place in my house for two I's."

MATHNAWI

The Rose Garden Has Flowered

ONE DAY our Master stopped in the marketplace. All the inhabitants of the town were present. The Master turned his face from the people towards a wall, while going on teaching mystical precepts. At the moment of evening prayer, when night fell, the dogs of the market formed a circle around him. He threw them loving and holy looks and continued his explanations. The dogs shook their heads and tails, moaning gently in rapture. Rumi said, "I swear by God, that these dogs understand our gnosis. This door and this wall too proclaim the praises of God and understand the divine mysteries."

> Where is the Eye able to see souls
> Where others can see only 'door' and 'wall'?
> 'Door' and 'wall' are always subtle things:
> Fire, earth, water—all tell sublime stories.

At once, the Friends started to appear from all sides. The Master called out, "Come, the Supreme Friend has come; come, the rose garden has flowered!"

AFLAKI

O Most Glorified One!
O Most Holy One!

ONE DAY Sheikh Sadr-ed-din, the Qadi Siraj-ed-din, and other scholars, dervishes, and mystics, had left Konya to go and contemplate the great mosque of Meram and its gardens; our Master had agreed to join them.

After a while, Rumi got up and went into a mill, where he stayed a long time. Hours went by. At last the Sheikh and the Qadi set out to look for him. They went into the mill and saw him busy with a ritual dance before the mill wheel.

"In the name of God," Rumi cried out. "Tell me if it isn't true that this mill wheel is saying Sobbouh! Qoddous! (O most glorified one! O most holy one!)"

The Sheikh told us what followed, "At that moment, the Qadi and I heard, with our own physical ears, that these words were in fact coming from the mill wheel."

Rumi then began to recite this ghazal:

> The heart is like a grain
> And we're like the mill wheel;
> Does the mill wheel know
> Why it turns and keeps turning?
> Our body's like the mill wheel,
> Our thoughts are the water
> That makes it turn and turn.

The mill wheel speaks out
And the water knows what's happened.
The water says, 'Ask the miller
Who throws this water down the hill?
The miller will tell you, O bread lover
If the wheel didn't turn
Who could be a baker?.'
Many adventures will unravel. Silence!
Ask God so He can tell you them.

We went into ecstasy contemplating the marvelous greatness of what our Master was describing. When we came back to ourselves, he had disappeared.

AFLAKI

She Was Always Referring to Him

Zuleikha applied to Joseph the name of every single
   thing,
From a grain of celery to a branch of aloe.
She hid his name under all other names, and only let
Her special confidantes into the secret.
When she said, "The wax's being melt by the fire,"
That meant "My beloved's madly in love with me."
When she said, "Look, the moon is up" or
"The branch of the willow's green again"
Or if she said, "The leaves are trembling passionately,"
Or "The rose has told its secret to the nightingale,"
Or "The King has revealed his passion for Shahnaz,"
Or "How lucky things seem!" or "Shake the dust from the
   furniture,"
Or "The water carrier's here" or "The sun is risen!"
Or if she said, "Yesterday evening we cooked a lot of food,"
Or "The vegetables are perfectly done,"
Or if she said, "The bread has no taste whatsoever,"
Or "The heavenly sphere turns in a contrary direction,"
Or "I have a headache" or "My migraine is better,"
She was always referring to him, always speaking of Joseph.
If she ever praised anything, it was always to sing
Of the tenderness of the caresses of Joseph:
Whenever she blamed or cursed anything, it was always

To speak of the agony of separation from him.
Whenever she was hungry, she had only to say his name
To feel full and drunk from its radiant cup.
Whenever she was thirsty, Joseph's name slaked her thirst:
Just saying his name was sorbet for her soul.
And if she suffered, her suffering became acceptance
As soon as his name had sounded in her heart.
When it grew cold, Joseph's name was her fur.
This is what the name of the Beloved can do
When you are truly and finally lost in love.
When the soul has truly been united to God
To speak of God is to speak of the soul
And to speak of the soul is to speak of God.

MATHNAWI

Why Would I Not Be Honest?

THERE WAS a scholar monk, from the country around Constantinople, who had heard of the knowledge, sweetness, and humility of our Master. Full of affection for Rumi, although he was of a different religion, he set out and arrived at Konya looking for him. The monks of Konya went to meet him and received him with honor. He then asked to visit Rumi, and met him by chance on the road. The monk prostrated three times before him. When he rose up he saw that Rumi had also prostrated himself; it is said that he bowed his head thirty-three times to the monk. Crying out loud and tearing his robe, the monk exclaimed, "O sultan of religion! How can you take to such an extreme point the humiliation and self-abasement you show me, who am just a miserable wretch full of faults!" Rumi replied, "Our Prophet gave us the following *hadith*: 'Happy is he whom God gave wealth, beauty, honor, and power and who has been generous in his wealth, chaste in his beauty, humble in his honor, just in his power.' How could I not be humble before the servants of God, and why would I not be honest and show my own misery and nothingness? If I did not, what would I be useful for?"

AFLAKI

The Highest Rank

W<small>HILE THE IMAGE</small> of the Friend burns in our thought,
The whole of our life flows in contemplation.
Wherever union with the Friend exists,
There is, in the middle of the house, a flowering garden.
Wherever the heart reaches its goal,
A thousand dates are worth less than a single thorn.
When we sleep near the dwelling of the Friend,
Our bed and the blankets over us are the Pleiades.
When I fall asleep, mingled in the hair of the Friend,
I hold the highest rank in the Night of Destiny.
When the reflection of His beauty flames out,
The mountains and earth become silk and brocade.
When I beg His fragrance from the wind,
It carries to me the sounds of lute and oboe.
When I write His name in the dust,
Each grain of dust becomes an angel.
When in His name I say a magical spell on the fire,
Through Its power the blaze transforms into water.
Why go on speaking? When even before Nothingness
I say His name, He bestows existence.
The subtlest thought about his Love
Is denser than the heaviest kernel.
At the moment that Love manifests,

Everything we know or see faints away.
Keep silent now; see, all things are dissolving;
The supreme Goal is the Lord Himself.

ODES

Paradox on Paradox

WHEN THE PROVISION of the Invisible has become
  your food,
You've won Eternal Life and death has fled.
When the agony of love has begun to expand your life,
Roses and lilacs take over the garden of your soul.
What terrifies others is your deepest security:
The river that exhausts the turkey makes the duck strong.
Once again, Doctor, Your cure has driven me mad!
Once again, I've lost my mind in Your Glory!
Paradox on paradox; the rings of your chains are endless!
And each ring engenders a different kind of madness!

MATHNAWI

What Is This Sacred Dance?

Is it an army of angels that is stirring this tumult?
Are these cascades of laughter from those who live in
    heaven?
What is this sacred dance all souls are dancing?
What is this whistle that brings all hearts flying?
Who is this young bride and how rich is her dowry
That heaven itself becomes her nuptial dais?
Look, the moon's bringing us a plate heaped with gold
    coins.
What is the prey the arrow of Destiny pierces?
And if it hasn't struck, why does the bow moan?
Happy news, lovers! Dance and clap your hands!
The one who escaped us has returned in rapture!
The heights of heaven's wall ring with the cry: "Have
    mercy!"
From the shores of the ocean arrive the flood of divine
    truths.
The eyes of Fortune are astounded by your happiness:
That shows it flames out in every direction.
You've escaped at long last this world of famine
Where long bitter struggle wins only scraps of bread.
What is nobler than the soul? Yet, when it leaves, don't
    mourn:
Something even more precious will take its place.

How can I—or anyone else—ever cease being astounded
That He whom nothing can contain is contained in the
heart?

The Voluntary Slave

IN ALL THE EARTHS and heavens, not an atom moves
   a wing
Nor a straw trembles, except by His eternal order.
No one can explain this, and no one should try—
Who can count all the leaves on the trees?
How can the Infinite become the object of words?
Since every action arrives because of God's decree
When the predestination of God becomes his servant's joy
He becomes the voluntary slave of His decree.
Not by conformity, and not because he wants a reward,
But because his entire nature has become purified.
Such a person does not desire his life for himself
Nor does he hanker after the glory of a life to come:
Living and dying are for him the same thing.
He lives for the love of God; he dies for the love of God
And not out of any fear or any suffering.
He does not hunger for the trees and streams of Paradise:
His faith is perfect in his passion to do God's will.

MATHNAWI

His Rarer Alchemy

THERE WAS A concert one evening in the palace of Perwane Moin-ed-din, the Grand Chamberlain of Konya; sheikhs and important people were present. Our Master seemed to be disturbed and uttered cry after cry; finally, he went into a corner of the house and stood there. After a moment, he ordered those reciting not to say another word. Everyone was stupefied; after a while, he lifted up his head; his two eyes had become two pools of blood. He then cried out "My friends, come closer and contemplate in my eyes the greatness of the divine lights." No one could do so; those who tried to look found their eyes misted over or weak; the friends cried out in despair and lowered their heads.

Our Master then turned his gaze to Tchelebi Hosam-ed-din and said to him, "Come, my religion and my faith! Come to me, my soul! Come, my King!" Tchelebi started to moan and weep. Then the Perwane glanced secretly at Khorasani and said to him, "Look, can what our Master said about Tchelebi Hosam-ed-din really be true?"

Immediately Tchelebi came forward and seized the Perwane and said to him, "O Emir, even if it was not true before, the moment the Master said it was it became so, and I became what he said I am. His order when he wants anything consists uniquely in saying *be* and it is."

Tchelebi then recited these verses:

> His action is expressed by these words *"be"* and it is;
> It does not depend on second causes

And he added: "It is well known through alchemy a piece of brass becomes gold; his rarer alchemy has made of my brass the philosopher's stone."

AFLAKI

Divine Pride

ONE DAY, someone asked Rumi, "We see that certain ancient sages were extremely proud—what does such pride mean?"

He replied, "In people of God, pride is a pride of divine greatness, and not a pride of opinions or passion, nor a presumption that arises from high spiritual rank. When the Imam Dja'far Cadiq, who purified his soul and paid no attention to caliphs and Kings, was asked about this pride, he replied, "I myself am not proud. I have abandoned my own existence, the greatness of God has annihilated me and installed itself in place of my pride; the pride I am speaking of springs directly out of the heart of the greatness of God; as for me, in the middle of all this glory, I do not exist."

AFLAKI

You Will Not Hear One from Me

ONE DAY, our Master was passing through one of the districts of Konya; two strangers were quarreling and saying terrible things to each other. Rumi stopped at some distance from them and heard one say to the other, "Don't you know who you are speaking to? If you say another word, you'll hear a thousand in reply!" Rumi then approached the sparring couple, "No, come to me, and pour out to me all the words you have on your mind, because even if you have ten thousand of them, you will not hear one from me." The two enemies fell at his feet and made peace immediately.

AFLAKI

God Wears Red

Fᴀᴋʜʀ-ᴇᴅ-ᴅɪɴ Aᴅɪʙ, one of the best of the friends, told us that one day the Master, in the middle of a large meeting, commented dazzlingly on this *hadith* of the Prophet. "I have only seen God wearing a red robe." No one could say a word as he spoke; everyone was amazed by what he said. He recited this poem spontaneously:

> In the middle of the red threads of this robe
> There is a light higher than all eyes, than any spirit.
> If you want to sew for yourself a robe like this,
> Get up now and tear in shreds the veil of passion.
> The spirit has taken on bodily form—the Prophet's—
> Has become his eyelids, his eyes, his brown
>   complexion:
> Inexplicably, the Godhead has taken on the form
> Of the Prophet Mohammed, the Chosen One.
> This form's really the vanishing of all form:
> His narcissus eyes blaze with the Day of Resurrection.
> When the physical form of the Prophet was withdrawn,
> The world began to murmur, "Allah is great! Allah is
>   great!"
> Every time this form gazed out in love at the Creation,
> A hundred thousand doors were flung open by God.

Then Rumi explained that in dream symbolism to be dressed in a red garment means ecstasy and joy, green denotes ascesis, white the fear of God, and blue and black signify mourning and grief.

AFLAKI

Go Further Always

ONE DAY, the story of Sheikh Kermani was told our Master. The Sheikh loved to dally with beautiful boys, but in all honor, because he did nothing with them. Rumi cried out, "Would to God that he *had* done something and gone beyond it all!" Our Master used to say:

> O my brother, the royal court is infinite:
> Whatever comes to you, go further always—
> Never remain in the same place.

AFLAKI

The Direct View

ONE DAY, in the service of our Master, a person said, "All the prophets and spiritually advanced beings have trembled before the terror and torments of death." Our Master replied, "God keep us from feeling like them! Do people have any idea what death is? Death, for mystics, is the direct view of Supreme Truth; why would they flee from such a vision?"

AFLAKI

My Burial Ground Will Invite You to Dance

If FROM my dust wheat springs
And you make bread from this wheat, it'll make you drunk.
Both dough and baker will become mad
And the oven will sing songs of drunkards.
If you come in pilgrimage to my tomb,
My burial ground will invite you to dance:
My brother, don't come without a tambourine
There's no seat for grief at the Feast of God.
Death sleeps in the ground, its jaws bound tightly,
It has fallen down drunk from the opium of the Friend.
When you tear off this shroud and match it to your height,
You'll discover a wine shop in your own soul:
From all sides will ring an ecstatic tumult of lutes.
Doesn't every action necessarily breed its effect?
God has created me from the wine of love;
I am that love itself, although death has made me dust.
I am drunkenness, my essence is this mystic wine.
Tell me then, what breeds wine if not drunkenness?
Around and around the tower of the spirit of Shams of
    Tabriz
My soul keeps on and on flying without stopping a moment.

ODES

Stage After Stage

In the beginning, when man was nonexistent, God brought him into existence. Then God took him through stage after stage—from sheer existence into the inanimate world, from there into the vegetable world, from the vegetable world into that of the animal, from the animal to the human, from the human to the angelic world, and so on and on forever. Why did God manifest all of these amazing transformations? So we can all be certain that He has many further stages each more exalted than the other.

You will certainly traverse stage after stage—

What is the matter with you that you do not believe?

Why did God unveil this world we are in now? So you have to acknowledge the thousands of other stages that stretch ahead infinitely. God did not unveil this world simply to have you wallow in disbelief and proclaim, "This is all there is!"

A master craftsman demonstrates his skill and artfulness so his apprentices can entrust their faith to him, and believe in the other arts he has not exhibited. A King bestows robes of honor and presents and treats his subjects with extravagant benevolence so they can look forward to receiving other blessings from him and can await in hope other gifts of gold. He does not give them all he does so they can say, "This is all there is. The King is not going to bestow on us anything else," and so they make do with what they have. If the King knew that was what his subjects would say, he would never give them blessings and gifts in the first place.

TABLE TALK

Become a Sea

Every form you see draws its origin from the unseen divine world. So if the form vanishes, what does it matter? Its origin was from the Eternal. Do not grieve that every form you see, every mystical truth you hear will one day vanish. The Fountain is always gushing water. Neither Fountain nor the water will ever stop flowing, so why mourn? Your spirit is a fountain; river after river flow from it, put all mourning out of your mind forever and keep on drinking from the water. Do not be afraid. The water is limitless.

When you came into this world of created beings, a ladder was placed before you, so that you might climb out of it. At first, you were inanimate; you then became a plant; after that, you were transformed into an animal. At long last, you transmuted into a human being, imbued with knowledge, intelligence, and faith. Next, you will become an angel. Then you will have finished this world and your dwelling will be in the Light-world of Heaven. Go beyond even that, go beyond even the station of an angel. Pass into that vast Ocean, so that the single drop—yourself—can become a Sea.

Odes

On the First Day of Every Year

On the first day of the Arab new year, our Master used to recite the following prayer at the moment when the crescent moon was first glimpsed. "O great God, You are the Eternal One both in the past and in the future! This is a new year; I beg You to be protected against Satan and to be helped to fight against the greedy and lustful soul in me that orders me to do evil, to busy myself with things that draw me closer to You, and avoid those that pull me away from You. O God, kind and merciful one! I ask You this in the name of Your Pity, Magnanimous and All-generous One!"

AFLAKI

Look for the District of Joy

SULTAN VALAD, our Master's son, recounted: "One day I said to my father, 'The friends claim that when they do not see you it causes them pain and their inner joy disappears.' My father replied, 'Whoever does not feel joyful in my absence does not really know me; the one who really knows me feels happy even without me; he will be suffused with me, with the thought of me, with my thought.' He added, 'Every time, my son, that you find yourself in a state of mystic sweetness know that this state is me in you.'" Sultan Valad added, "This is why my father used to say,

> When you look for me, look in the district of joy:
> We are the inhabitants of the world of joy.

AFLAKI

United Tenderly

You are glorified in heaven, O subtle Sun!
Be glorified now on earth for eternity!
May the inhabitants of earth become one in their hearts,
Unite their plans and designs with the dwellers in heaven!
All separation and polytheism and duality will vanish
For there's only unity in real existence!
When my spirit recognizes your spirit fully,
Then the two of us remember being one before
And we become on earth like Moses and Aaron,
Heart-brothers united tenderly like honey and milk.

MATHNAWI

Reciprocal Loves

WHEN OUR GUIDES and those who are cherished by us leave and disappear, they are not annihilated. They are like stars that vanish into the light of the Sun of Reality. They exist by their essence and are made invisible by their attributes.

This subject has no end. If all the seas of the world were ink, and all the trees of all the forests were pens, and all the atoms of the air were scribes, still they could not describe the unions and reunions of pure and divine souls and their reciprocal loves.

LETTERS

SOURCES

Aflaki's *Biographies of the Mystics*
Letters
Odes
What Is in It Is in It: Rumi's Table Talk
Mathnawi

[All re-creations are mine.—Andrew Harvey]

GLOSSARY

QIBLA—Prayer niche in a mosque in the direction of Mecca

HADITH—Oral sacred saying of the Prophet, recorded either by one of his wives or by others of his intimate circle